WITH BREAST EXPANDED

BRIAN BEHAN

With Breast Expanded

LONDON
MACGIBBON & KEE
MCMLXIV

FIRST PUBLISHED 1964 BY MACGIBBON & KEE LTD
COPYRIGHT © BRIAN BEHAN 1964
PRINTED IN GREAT BRITAIN BY
THE GARDEN CITY PRESS LTD
LONDON AND LETCHWORTH

This book I dedicate to money
and flat-chested women

CONTENTS

7

Part I

Part 1

CHAPTER ONE

Uncle Paddy

MY UNCLE PADDY always wore his cap in bed; a greasy black thing, he would use it to whack my brother Sean. 'Up with the lark, Boy' he would cry. This was at 11 o'clock in the morning, time by which Padner judged the streets were well aired and fit for Christian activity. My brother had to suffer his company in our bed because my mother was entertaining Paddy in the hopes that he might part with some cash—in fact, he never gave us a light. His cap wasn't his only claim to fame. He was pursued night and day by two women, Mary Grist and Nanny Waters. Both these girls lusted after the bold Padner. The fact that he stood to inherit my Granny's three tenement-houses may have had something to do with it. There were other rumours mainly spread by the league of disgruntled fat men, to the effect that like all skinny men, Padner was unreasonably well-endowed. Of this, I had no proof either way, but he was skinny enough and if big whats'its do go with small, skinny men then truly he was a champion.

The Dublin slums produce two types of men. One breed is short, butty and thickset. The pick of the crop, these are the ones who through generations have laughed at dirt and disease. Immune to chicken-pox or measles they thrive on fresh air and potatoes. They turn into coal-heavers and door-men for Arthur Guinness. The other is a thin, weedy mixture that should have gone with the other puny things to the grave. Such a one was Paddy. Whether through shame or guilt, the women will die for the weaker half and ignore the bully. Paddy's mother worshipped the ground he walked on. Work, she considered too hard for him and kept him at home to look after the 'property.' Even with three houses, this wasn't a very big task. Over two hundred years old, my Granny just let them rot on to corporation condemnation. She despised her tenants and thought she honoured them by allowing them to pay her rent. Every year, the houses be-

11

came more and more over-crowded, until, in some, thirteen families were using a lavatory made for two. Paddy's biggest problem was blocked and broken bowls. To help him in his freemasonry he engaged me and my brother Sean as lavatory-divers with ninepence a time for each bowl cleared. This was all right until one day I went with him to clear one and found a screaming woman outside the lavatory door.

'Ah,' she roared, 'the dirty baste he's robbing my poor daughter's virginity. For God's sake stop him!' It appeared that Ballock the Boar (who later won renown by chasing his father up and down the road with a hatchet) was busy within raping the woman's daughter. I must say, in view of the rape, she was keeping remarkably quiet. Paddy in a flurry, banged on the door.

A voice roared 'Who's there?'

Paddy timidly replied, 'It's me.'

The voice came back, 'I don't know anyone called me. Away off and leave me alone. Can't a man drop his trousers in peace anymore.'

At this, the woman became frenzied; 'You lying animal, you have my poor daughter in there. Let her go or I'll be dug out of you.' The door flew open; but like the girl in the magician's box, she had vanished.

'Now,' growled Ballock, 'are you satisfied or is it a good view of the ins and outs of my arse you're after?' Stupefied, the woman could only stand there with her gaping maw open. I spotted the loose planks at the back of the lavatory but thought I had better say nothing.

The next day I went up to my Granny's room to see if I could get a couple of coppers for doing a message. As always, Paddy's rival suitors, Nanny and Mary, were there. When Paddy was about his business they would compete for his hand by plying his mother with food. Since the weedy Paddy was indifferent to food they had come to the conclusion that the way to his heart was through his mother's stomach. She herself was bedridden and sometimes she would get me to read to her from the *Oracle*. As I came to the wickedness of nurse Baron trying to poison the heroine she would cry, 'Oh the dirty thing.' I would stop and look up.

To the other two she would cry, 'Ah, it's lucky the poor boy doesn't know what he's reading.'

The atmosphere between the two cooks was far from cordial and I used to try to ignore their quarrels by looking out of the window. Down below, I could see the canal that divided our street from the better class, tradesmen's district. Here we swam and tried to build dams. Once I tried to walk to the end of the canal and finally gave up in the dead of night about ten miles away. The eternal source of entertainment, we waited until the barges came either puffing on their little engines or pulled by huge, bony horses. Then we would leap onto them from the bank and dive off the end, much to the annoyance of the bargees and the horror of our mothers, who were forever telling us about boys being sucked under and never seen again or having their heads chopped off by the propellers.

Ballock was our canal hero. Big and strong, he spent his days doing somersaults into the middle and splashing and snorting like some crazy Tarzan. He didn't believe in work but reserved his strength for his other, more important pursuit, women.

One great thing about the slums was the hordes of children. We played in gangs of twenty and thirty all night long till the cries of the different mothers rang out: 'Kevin,' 'Brian,' 'Tommy, get in here or I'll get your da to you.' One thing sure—you were never short of a group to play in.

From my Granny's window I could see the cellars opposite where we played 'fathers and mothers' or hospitals, or sometimes someone would suggest 'horses and mares.' These games made sex-education quite unnecessary.

Behind me in the room the two young women were getting more and more heated. They were supposed to be making pancakes but were falling out over whose turn it was to stir the mixture. My Granny raised herself up in bed, her long black hair giving her a witch-like appearance.

'Ah, for heavens sake, what does it matter who stirs it.' But the cooks had forgotten her. Each now had a hand on the spoon and was trying to turn it in the opposite direction. Great dollops of batter were flying out in all directions. In a fury Mary seized the bowl and crashed it upside-down on Nanny's head. As soon as she could see,

Nanny started to look round for some implement with which to beat her foe. Terrified, Mary made for the stairs. But alas, her enemy had found a suitable weapon and quick as a flash poured over her what my Granny was to describe to a neighbour as 'common nuisance, Mam. She grabbed a bucket of common nuisance from under my bed and drowned that poor wan in it.'

Everyone in the street agreed that round went to Nanny. How and ever Mary must have got an edge on her, for one day as I was helping my mother hang out the washing, Paddy came tearing by pursued by Nanny. She was laughing and crying and calling out to Paddy to stop. But she had an open razor in her hand and Paddy kept on running. When he disappeared round the corner she stopped and resting her head against the bricks she sobbed and moaned and then just as my mother began to move towards her, she straightened up and slowly drew the razor across her neck. I thought she must be play-acting, but two red lips opened in her throat and I hid my face in my mother's skirt.

I went to see Paddy years after, in Blessington Street. All I saw was his peak cap. He was in his nightshirt and as I made to come in I thought I saw the form of a woman vanish up the stairs. It might have been the half-light of a tenement-hall.

CHAPTER TWO

Funerals

WHEN my Granny died they called me in to see her. I hesitated at the door and wouldn't go in. It was so dark in there. All I could see were some candles throwing shadows back on the heavy velvet curtains that reached down to the ground. I shrank back against my mother and heard a woman say: 'Ah, don't force him to go in, Mam, sure he doesn't understand there's no harm in the poor woman.'

She was wrong. I understood only too well. My Granny had ceased to be a big black-haired woman and was now a waxy-faced image that stared out at nothing and yet everything. She knew more than me now. The dead always seemed to me to have an advantage over the living. They have done something we have yet to go through. In the slums, because we were so packed together, people seemed to be dying all the time. It was either the very old or the very young. The very young presented no problem. Wrapped in a clean shawl they were put carefully into a rude wooden box. Then up on their daddy's shoulder they took their last piggy-back to the cold cloddy earth. With the older people it was different.

To drive away the god, death, wakes were held at which the living intoned the goodness of the one gone before. Now in the face of death even Satan, the first great rebel, came in for his share. 'Ah, God is a good man, and the devil is not a bad fella when he's treated right.'

Once my father and a friend went to a wake and decided to liven the thing up. The dead man had been a hunchback and in death as in life he was almost sitting up in the coffin. Lifting him out my father put him sitting with his cap on at the top of the dimly-lit tenement stairs. To add to the effect, they lifted his arm up and left it pointing straight down to Old Nick. Two women came sighing up the stairs determined to pay their first, and last, respects to the dead. Then one of them halted for breath and looked up the stairs. Seeing her stop the other went on: 'Ah, Mrs, he was a jewel of a man, a living jewel.' The other just grabbed her arm and whispered:

'May the cross of Jesus be about us, Man, but look up there.'

'Oh God in heaven Mrs Julin darlin' but it's poor old Cruck.'

'Oh Mrs, the heart's cross-ways in me, in the name of God, let's get back down the stairs.'

'Stand your ground Biddy Fitz. Aren't you a Catholic, or what? What harm can poor old Cruck do us now? I will soon see if it's the devil disguised as Cruck or if it's a friendly spirit. God in heaven, wasn't it lucky I brought this jar of Holy Water with me.' Then lifting up the jar and flinging it over Cruck she called out, 'In the name of the Father, Son and Holy Ghost.'

My father's mate had fallen asleep in drink behind Cruck and as the cold water splashed across his face he woke up roaring: 'Who the fuckin' hell is throwing all the water about. Fuck off, or by Jesus I will swing for ye.' Screaming, the poor women dived down the stairs out into the street.

My Granny specified when she died that they must be black, fat horses that pulled her hearse. She wanted no skinny ones. I went to her funeral and felt I was really somebody of importance. I went round proudly telling the other kids, 'My Granny's died and I'm having a day off school to go to the funeral.' All the horses had great big, black feathers rising up out of their heads. The chief mourners' coach was pulled by a fine black pair. It was a fat, round coach that looked much better than the brown, narrower coaches pulled by one old nag. In these travelled the not-so-close, and then bringing up the rear walked those who couldn't afford to have a coach or share one. One thing was certain, there wasn't a dry throat by the time the coach rached Glasnevin cemetery. We stopped at the Brian Boru Bar and drank and drank before we turned to the road that leads back to the centre of Dublin.

Of course, for years my mother died every week. Regularly she would collapse and beg us to send for the doctor. Once she was so far gone we even had the priest in to give extreme unction. And she enjoyed every death-bed scene. On one occasion about twenty years ago I heard her clasp my dad's hand and beg him: 'Look after Sean, Frank, give me your word you will.'

But three minutes later she was springing about like a leopard.

A couple of years ago she came to London and was met off the train by Henry Fielding of the *Daily Herald*. In our house she sat as demure as a deb while they took photos and interviewed her. The reporter had his angle all ready, 'Meet Mrs Behan; an ordinary little old lady; could be anyone's dear old mum.' Then suddenly to the poor man's astonishment she started to roar out the 'Red Flag' and do a wild dance with her skirts flying. That night she was to appear on *Tonight*. The interviewer had already run over her answers with her in a little rehearsal. He passed over Don and Brendan all right but when he came to me the question went: 'And now Mrs Behan, what about your son Brian, didn't you have a lot of trouble with him as a child?' This I suppose was an attempt to trace my union-activities back to juvenile delinquency. My mother hadn't quite weighed up the situation and, wanting to be obliging, she answered: 'Oh yes, I did.'

The dirty louses, I thought, taking advantage of an old woman. After the run through they took her up to the studio for the broadcast and we watched it downstairs. On came my mother and away went the interviewer. Everything went according to plan, until: 'And now Mrs Behan, your son Brian, didn't you have a lot of trouble with him as a boy?'

'Not at all, he was one of the best boys I ever reared. I hear he's causing a lot of strikes over here and more power to his elbow.' She turned to the interviewer, 'Sure the working man never got anything without fighting for it, did he?'

The stricken man could only smile wanly and say what a wonderful woman she was.

CHAPTER THREE

Me Ma and Da

'MY MOTHER is a great big tall woman. My Da is not so tall but he is very fat.' It was 1933 and I was writing a composition about my parents. I was seven years old and my ma and da were the whole world. Without them my happiness would have collapsed into the sad, bitter little pilgrimage of the orphans that passed our door on their Sunday walks.

My mother wasn't really very tall but her leanness made her appear so. She had very thick, powerful arms; heavily veined from countless runs up and down the scrubbing board. A mountain of energy she was forever scootering somewhere. A proud woman, she always told me to ignore what other people thought or said about me. 'Ask yourself, are they going to give you anything? If not, take no notice of them.'

Once infected by anti-Jewry from school, I pointed to a little Jewish boy and said 'Look Mammy, there's a dirty Jewish Jew.' She said nothing but drew out and whacked me right across the mouth. 'Now never call anyone a dirty anything again,' she said, 'they're all some poor mothers' sons!'

In our street all the women sat out on the tenement steps in the long summer evenings, where they would stay for hours on end. My mother would not let me sit with them so they started to call her Lady Behan and tried to make her life a misery. She pretended not to notice but my father, no gentleman and certainly no lady, went for them. My father was one of them in a sense. He was as Dublin as the hills, and knew how to talk to them so that they left my mother alone.

'My father is a very jolly man,' I wrote then, and it's just as true today. He always claims he's in his prime and getting better. I dread to think what we'll do with him when he's a hundred. Tie him down I suppose, or shoot him. As it is, I have to watch him very carefully when he starts embracing his daughters-in-law. His welcoming hugs have to be seen to be believed. But yes, a jolly man. I have never seen

18

him strike one of us or raise his voice to my mother. He always wore a good-natured grin, whatever the trouble he had to face; maybe that's why his work-mates called him Rosy; because he was red-faced, small and butty like a rosy apple.

One fearfully cold day in December I brought his lunch to the job he was on; it was outside work and his hands were frozen stiff from trying to concentrate on painting a sign thirty foot up. Yet when he came down the ladder he was the same old Da. Pipe going full blast, he said, 'There you are me old segoia, good lad.' If there is any genius in the Behans it springs from my father's earthy, good humour crossed with my mother's energy and determination.

My mother was fresh-air mad. This was probably due to the fact that she is a peasant once removed. All her people come from Rath-maiden in the County Meath. At the first sign of sun, she would tear round getting us all ready and whip us off to the sea or park. Those first ten years of my life, from 1926 to 1936, were among the happiest I have ever known. Of course, I had bad moments; being shy and sensitive, other boys delighted in teasing and thwarting me. One day, one of my brothers and another boy started ribbing and prodding me like a bullock in a stall. Unfortunately for them, deep in my blood I had my mother's ferocious temper, and driven almost mad I grabbed up a piece of rock and smashed it down on the boy's thigh, almost crippling him.

Fortunately for the family, my father was so gentle by nature that you would nearly have to kill him before he would take any notice. But anything that touched us had an immediate effect on him. Once, I was lying very ill and our next-door neighbour started playing the piano. Twice my mother asked him to stop and let me rest. He ignored her and played on. When my father came and my mother told him what was going on he threw down his knife and fork and darted out to see Cruck Reilly, the owner of the piano. Diving into the room he grabbed the piano and started to heave it towards the window, the startled Cruck hanging onto the other end for dear life. My father shouted, 'If you don't stop playing this fucking piano, it's going out of the window and you with it.' The much-chastened Cruck abandoned his piano practice.

As far as my father was concerned, the sun never shone on anything better than us. My mother was the same, a terribly loyal woman;

if anything or anybody touched her lambs she went for them like a she-wolf. Once, in school, a young nun called me out and smacked me very hard on the face. When I told my mother, she immediately threw on her coat and hat swearing vengeance. 'But Mammy,' I protested 'you can't hit a holy nun.' But she hadn't heard, she was striding down the road to William Street school. I don't know what happened when she got there, but I remember lessons were very peaceful for me from then on.

There were six of us boys in the family and I remember we had to sleep four to a bed, two each end. The problem in sleeping like this is to avoid the other fella's feet and to make sure you got in the middle position, not hanging off the edge with no covers.

There's a silly slander that used to go round about the Irish keeping pigs in their kitchen. I never saw that though I once knew a woman who kept a donkey in her back room. A widow woman she was, who kept herself by selling coal. In the bitter cold weather she used to take long-eared Neddy up the stairs for a warm. One night we were playing 'spirits' in our bedroom, a game in which we pretended the old gas brackets that jutted over the fireplace were magic telephones that could put us in touch with Santa Claus or anyone else we fancied. We had just finished giving our list and posting a little letter to go with it up the chimney, when we heard a terrible clatter of hooves outside the door. Startled out of our wits we dived straight under the blankets. The door slowly opened to admit a great shaggy, hairy head. Screaming now, we were convinced it was Old Nick, we roused our father. Only when we heard him asking Mrs Cavanagh to keep her effing donkey to herself did we realise who our visitor had been.

My father was always reading, but not just to himself. When they were both in bed, my mother would snuggle up behind him and coax him to read out loud to her. She couldn't read so well; she had had an injury to her eye when she was young, though, as she said herself, it didn't stop her getting two husbands where others couldn't manage to get one. When she was annoyed with Da for any reason she used to set up a long wail about Jack, her first husband, and give us a long cata-logue of his virtues. Da used to say 'Yes, yes, Kathleen, it was a sad day for me when he died.'

She blamed her bad eye on the surgeons, saying 'Remember, Brian, they practise on the children of the poor.' Not that she could avoid hospitals, with seven children all getting various infected ears and noses and broken limbs. She must have spent nearly half her life waiting in hospital corridors. And like any other woman, who has to manage on half nothing, she had her hard side. Once, when she didn't want to pay somebody waiting on the doorstep, I foolishly went to the door and said, 'Me Mammy says she's not in and even if she was she couldn't pay you till next week.' The collector wasn't quite satisfied and craned his neck round the door and caught my mother standing in the kitchen. She went for him hammer and tongue, calling down on him for not believing an innocent child, and daring to suggest that her child could be lying.

My mother always loved animals and couldn't bear to see anyone being cruel to stray cats or dogs. Time and again she released some poor cat from its tormentors and soundly boxed their ears. Once, she brought in a pup off the stairs and reared him by letting him lap out of her hand. 'Failte' (Welcome) we called him. He was brown and shaggy, a three-quarter terrier. We loved him and it seemed we were all to keep him for years. But soon my mother told us he would have to go. Some neighbours had complained that he was biting their kids. I didn't believe it; he had never bitten any of us, but despite my tears, he was taken off to the dogs' home for execution. Half way there Failte must have become suspicious for he darted off and no amount of entreaty could bring him back. After two weeks of seemingly endless searching, we got him back and I cried myself to sleep with him in my arms. But the damage was done, he never trusted us after that and kept running away. For years we kept seeing his form here, there and everywhere haunting us like an angry brown ghost.

CHAPTER FOUR

New Houses, Cold Comfort

IN OUR tenement basement, I was as happy as the flowers in May, although I know now that it was a time of hardship for my parents. There always seemed to be plenty of grub. Every Saturday, I would go with my mother to Moore Street to buy for the weekend. Here the dealers, arms bare, shouted 'Here, Mam!'—then, as my mother would make to walk on, they would run beside her saying, 'Ah now, Mam, looka these lovely oranges. Take these for luck, ah go on, Mam, these are the last three.' Crowded and jostled, we went to the butchers to buy a solid slab of corned or salt beef, as they say in England. Then on to the German shop for pork sausages and lovely brawn with seasoning sprinkled over each slice. By now, my mother's bag was fully packed with oranges and apples spilling over the top. For going with her, she would do me a tea, just the two of us, by the fire; then I felt like a king.

One day, she started to cry on the tram, and I asked her why. She told me she had opened a letter addressed to Brendan and telling him where to join a ship for Spain and the Civil War. She never gave him the letter. Our family was republican to the marrow of our bones; mother rocked us in the cradle to airs of rebel songs. She taught us that it was noble to hate your oppressors, but I'm glad to say that she was a mother first and a republican after.

Out in the streets, the hordes of kids played for hours until, through the long shadows, you heard the mothers calling, 'John Doyle, come in at once, d'ye hear me, I know you're there.' And Johnny would try and slope off and hide, desperate to get the last morsel out of the day, as if it were his last. We played such games as are possible only where large families are the rule. 'Every-Inch-a-Pinch' was my favourite game. One boy would rest his head and arms against the wall, and others would link arms behind him, making a causeway of bent backs. The test was to leap astride them and try to work your way up to the wall. Every time you moved the boys under you, they were entitled to pinch you as hard as they could. I was good at it because I'd be so mad to get to the wall and win that I didn't feel the pinches till after.

Slum clearance didn't just smash the houses, it smashed many a child. For me, hunger, loneliness and trouble dated from the hour that we went to the new housing estate. Here we knew nobody and those we found weren't the same somehow. Suddenly, we had to find ten bob rent every week, where before, like all the tenement dwellers, we had dodged paying the rent for years on the grounds that the places were falling down. Moreover, the 'planners' had omitted to include any schools and we had to pay bus fares to school every day. Was this all the left-Republican government of de Valera could offer? A little cold dogbox of a house and a shilling's worth of 'free beef.' All governments seem to amount to the same in the end. When all the screaming and shouting are done, what have you left but a load of fat-arse politicians in the snugs of public houses. Maybe, we should have stayed with the British, at least they would have had to keep us, and we would have fared better on their dole than on ours.

It's terrible to see how the biggest tyrannies seem to arise from the so-called revolutions. Freedom is a myth, a miasma, or, as my old mate Reg would put it, a load of balls. The looters of 1916 had a damn sight more sense than the fighters. If there is ever another war, I shall become a looter and get myself a country mansion from which I can denounce the Establishment, and from which I shall fight for home rule for the monkeys of Upper Jumbo.

I'm sure that de Valera pulled down our slums only to break up the anarchistic blocks of people who lived so communally that they ofttimes found themselves in one another's beds. Being such a solid crew, they paid neither tax nor rent, but managed to live by helping one another the best they could, and when things got tight, a little robbing in the rich world outside would help to fill empty bellies. No rent or tax man dared venture too deeply into our midst and the police preferred to leave us alone.

From our new house we wore a track to the pawn office. Everything seemed harsh, cold, miserable. To cap it all things in the building-game became tight. I was in a new school away from the kindly nuns and just went wild. I roamed here and there dodging school and gambling at pitch-and-toss. To get money for tossing, I stole from shops or from wherever I could get it. Finally, my bad school attendance plus petty thieving added up to an appearance at the Children's Court, and committal to Malin School. I had no fears of the Home. Tales of football-teas, boys' bands and the idea of a change of scene made me quite anxious to get there.

So one bright March day, I sat in a detective's car speeding up to the place where I was to spend the worst three years of my life. From the start I hated the place. The very first thing that they did was to strip me of my poor long pants and tog me out in a pair of short babyish ones. This initial stripping away of one's dignity is ritual, I have found, in every institution yet devised. In my new smallness I walked across the empty yard and into the refectory. Twelve hundred boys turned their heads to look me over. Red to the roots of my soul, I stumbled to my place, too miserable to eat. A little rat-faced boy next to me said: 'Will we help you eat your tea?' and away went my ration of bread and mug of cocoa.

CHAPTER FIVE

Malin

I MADE up my mind to run away. How far I could go or what I could do to keep alive I just couldn't figure out. One thing I was certain of—I hadn't the heart to go back with all the other boys.

There's nothing crueller than children, and complete savagery reigns among the children of the very poor. I would have died ten-times over rather than have them see me in my long trousers. All through the holidays they had become baggy and dirty. I had boasted before we left that I was getting a new suit to go back to school in. But all my mother bought me was a cheap pair of Oxford Bags from Clerys. Malin Reform School is run by the Christian Brothers, and it has been described by an American priest as a place 'where the rule of the boot and the fist still predominates.' And certainly I was aware of no shortage of either. Yet it wasn't the Brothers that led me to run away. It was the boys with their picking and pecking at any-one who seemed in the least bit different from the rest. All the first day I spent in the cinema watching the picture over and over again and when night came I made my way to a new housing estate and tried to sleep crouched in a doorway. The second night I spent in a Corporation dump. I managed to get into the back of an abandoned car and was snoring away when a hand shook me. It was a copper. 'Come on, son,' he said, 'time to go home.' At the police station I met my father: a small man, hurt and bewildered.

'What's the matter, son?'

I shrugged; I knew he wouldn't understand about the trousers, and, even if he did, there was nothing he could do about it.

A Brother came to collect me. He was the one the boys called 'monkey face.' He was kind, and the way back he chatted to me about this and that and the football team and what a silly boy I had been to run away. Unfortunately, he hadn't the last word in dealing with me. He was only the escort. In the dusk, we came up the drive; high on the hill, the square stone building looked down on the city. Lights were coming on in the dormitories but the Brother steered me into an empty classroom.

After about an hour two Brothers came in. One was Flint, the chief disciplinarian. The other was a Brother Grimes, his heir apparent. Grimes was a square man of six foot and about thirteen stone. I had never seen him smile. He had an impassive face like a Buddha. He hated nine-tenths of the twelve hundred boys committed to his care. 'City Jackeens,' he called them. Flint was an ex-policeman—a detective—it was said. He was taller than Grimes with an immense beaky nose. He smiled constantly; it was a dry old grin and sarcastic too; it was always used when he half-pulled your ear off in a friendly tug. 'You know what you are, boy?' he would smile, 'tell me now, what are you?' Trembling, the boy would keep his mouth shut, not knowing what to answer. 'You're a bowsey, boy, you hear me, a bowsey; you were put in here because you stole, because you couldn't keep your fingers to yourself, do you hear me?' Sometimes he tugged so hard that you brought your head right up with pain. With me, he had always been fair, kind even. Now he looked angry.

'Well,' he asked, 'why didn't you play honest Jack and come back with the rest, eh?'

I didn't answer. I just didn't know what to say. Moving round me, he kept talking.

'Well, you had to be a sneak. You couldn't come back with the rest, could you? Too much trouble, eh?'

Suddenly he lashed out and punched me straight in the mouth. As I went back I caught another from Grimes. The moment I moved to escape them, it seemed to set them off. Like greyhounds, they found it hard to hit something stationary, but let it move and it became a quarry. I suppose that if I had cried it would have saved me a lot of punching. I couldn't or wouldn't. So they beat me systematically. After a time they tired and told me to get up to my dormitory. First though they told me to wash my face in the horse trough.

Even in bed I was to have no peace. The master on duty was a Mr 'Frodge.' I never knew his real name. They called him Frodge because he wore the same pair of trousers winter or summer. These trousers, held up at half-mast, froze his ankles, thus Frodge. He resented my running away, and promptly set about whacking me in bed. To assist him in this holy task, he had a long thick stick which hurt me through the blankets. Then I cried because it seemed so unfair. Just when I thought I had had my beating, I had to go right through another. Frodge was one of a dozen poor teachers paid at a rate of a pound a week plus keep. For this they put in about seventy hours a week. Unlike the Christian Brothers, they had little or no religious inspiration to help them. They were just failures.

Years later I read on the back of a London lavatory door 'All big Irishmen are queers.' While there's some doubt about this, the Brothers did everything possible to make it a reality. They regarded sex as the biggest enemy since Luther. To drive out the foe they prescribed hard work, a covered body and a sound flogging, if they found anybody guilty of impurity. 'Impurity' covered everything from carnal activities to gentle daydreams. It was certainly true that we didn't get much time to ponder on the sexual problem.

You rose to the clap of Grimes' hand at six. You stripped to your waist and barefooted, winter or summer, you washed in freezing cold water. Hot pipes were, of course, an inducement to the devil and therefore couldn't be tolerated. Then quickly in and out of the lavatory: suitably divided cubicles of course; and then onto church. Praying was a big thing at Malin. Not satisfied with the praying of the priest, the Director would start the day with an hour from himself before Mass. We marched in our divisions from chapel to the refectory for breakfast. For meal-times the good Brothers had devised a means of control that would have put Stalin to shame. For a start, at the head of each table of twenty was a monitor. Each twenty was further sub-divided into five groups of four. Each four was allocated a loaf and a small dish of butter or dripping which they shared with scrupulous fairness. We used to heat the dripping over our tea and take turns at dipping our bread into it. To ensure absolute order, the whole one thousand two hundred moved to signals just like dogs. They blew a whistle and we said grace. They blew another and we sat, another and we were also allowed to begin eating but in complete silence. After ten minutes the whistle blew and we were permitted to talk; one more, and we stopped; one more, and we stood for grace; then a final blast sent us marching out to work or play. Yes, we did play. Football and handball were the main things, and there is no doubt that you would scarcely see a fitter lot outside the army.

Despite all precautions, sex did take place among the boys. How could it be otherwise among healthy human beings? In some cases, a boy who had been released might commit some trivial crime and be returned to the school for another year. Cock Connors—aptly named— was one of these. To us, he was a 'smoothy,' a boy well washed with his hair plastered down under a great weight of oil. He was a band boy. Unfortunately, he didn't confine his playing to purely musical instruments. Once a Brother was crossing the parade ground when he heard wild music coming from the band-room. Because there was no band practice due, and also attracted by the joyous tone, he decided to investigate. Inside, he saw four boys, bare as you like, dancing gaily about led by Connors playing like mad on his trumpet.

Apart from a shaven head and a birching, Connors seemed to get off fairly lightly. Two other sinners didn't fare so well, but then their crime was the worst in the book.

Occasionally, during play time, the chapel was packed. This didn't mean that the boys were consumed with a desire to pray, it simply meant that they were cold and that the chapel was the only place from the Brothers' quarters where there were hot pipes. So on freezing days, the boys dived into the chapel and pretended to trudge round the many stations of the cross. Ryan and Murphy must have got tired, for finding a sheltered niche behind a statue of the Blessed Virgin, they stopped and, according to the Director, acted like beasts of the field. He told us this at a specially convened mass rally the following morning. Our Director was a big imposing man. Stout without being fat or red in the face, he stood on the platform high above us and removed his tri-cornered hat with great solemnity. 'Boys,' he began, his voice thick with emotion; 'boys, I want you to look at these two miserable creatures. They may have the form of humans but they have the instincts of the lowest beasts. They have defiled their bodies in God's holy sanctuary. Yes, my sons,' his voice fell to a whisper, 'in God's holy sanctuary, in this month dedicated to His holy mother, the Blessed Virgin Mary. Now,' he roared, 'I want you to shun these boys as you would the Devil. For the next three months, no boy will contaminate himself by talking to them. You can draw a lesson from this.

These boys will be severely punished, you can rest assured of that. But what of their souls? We must all pray that God in his infinite mercy will find a way to forgive them.'

The two boys, one ten and one twelve years old, stood with heads bowed as the rest of us filed past. We didn't see them at all that day or the following night. When they at last appeared they were like two Belsenites, their heads shaven to the bone, each carrying a suitcase bearing the legend, 'I am impure, no boy should speak to me.'

All during the playtime they carried their pitiful burden round and round the parade ground. At first everyone watched and stood goggle-eyed. Then slowly but surely, they dropped into the accepted pattern, and were as much noticed as the big iron gates.

In pursuit of the enemy, the Brothers stopped up every bolt-hole. During the summer months, we were turned out into a twenty-acre field to play. Our longest playtime was a Saturday afternoon. For me, and others like me, football usually passed the time quite enjoyably. This particular day, it was too hot to move let alone kick about. We just wandered up and down the open field, but nowhere could we get any ease from the broiling sun. To sit down was a crime. To lie on the ground, the Brothers felt, was the door to sodomy. My mate on this day was a lad named McGuirk. Like fifty per cent of the boys there, he was a bastard. He paid over and over again for the sins of his father. He had been sent first of all to the nuns till he was four. Then he went to Malin till he was sixteen. The saddest thing of all was that these boys, knowing no other life, wept the night before they were due to leave. Indeed, some came back to work for life on the farm. On visiting days, the bastards sat with the others waiting for their fathers and mothers. Of course they never came. So they just sat there like little stones till the wind blew round an empty square.

I noticed McGuirk didn't look too well. As time went on he got paler and paler until I said, 'Sit down, Mac, you don't look too good.' At first he refused and only went down after I gently pressed him to the ground. I stood over him to give him as much shade as was pos-sible. Suddenly I was pushed aside and thin-lipped Frodge was looking down at him.

'Get up,' he barked.

'But, sir,' I said, 'he's not too well.'

Grinning Frodge asked me 'Ah, Behan, you're a doctor then?'

'No, sir,' I replied, 'but . . .'

'But nothing,' he shouted, 'seeing as you have so much to say, you can join McGuirk here in a nice trot round the field, and don't stop until I tell you.'

Round and round we went. After a second time round I began to feel a stitch in my side. Each time round I felt like stopping but the figure of Frodge kept me at it. McGuirk died in the March of the following year. T.B. he had, and they buried him in the tiny little bastards' graveyard at the back of the Brothers' house.

In every man there's a bit of a bully. My bit was knocked out in the baker's shop. There were six of us learning to be bakers. One of the boasts of Malin was that it gave boys a trade. This it did for about fifty per cent. The others went down on the farm under Bull Broderick. In addition to the farm there was a piggery with more than three hundred pigs. Then you had the fowl yard with dozens of hens. Yet in the three years I never ate an egg or a bit of a pig. Maybe the Brothers thought we were Moslems.

Every Brother on joining the Order took the name of a saint. The Brothers honoured each saint by celebrating his name day with a feast. As there were fifty Brothers, a feast day was one in every ten allowing for duplication. We always knew about these days as we had to prepare the cakes and bread for them. The Brothers, knowing that we weaker vessels couldn't withstand temptation, took a lesson from the workhouse master and abolished meat for evensong and morning meals. We starved the Devil with plain tea and bread and butter.

In the bakehouse, we didn't do so bad (which was one reason why I made straight for it). Working alongside me was a boy called Tague. As he had a slight stoop, the boys quickly christened him Humpy Tague. As I stooped over the mixing trough, I started to insult him. First I went on about his supposed hump and advised him to sandpaper it down. Then I told him I could lick him in fighting any day of the week. For a while he said nothing. Then quickly looking up he said, 'Right then, let's have a fight.' Frightened, I still had to follow him. As we made to go through the door into the storeroom, he suddenly turned and banged the door in my face. Half blinded, I staggered around until he took my arm and threw me on the ground. Here he seized me by the hair and began banging my head on the floor. Luckily, a couple of boys pulled him away before he had time to kill me.

I left Malin without any of the long preliminaries of the other boys. I was just getting a sponge when the supervisor told me, 'You're wanted in the head office.' I never saw him again. An old Brother told me that my father had secured my release before my time. I walked down the drive armed against the world with a prayer book and a large string of rosary beads.

CHAPTER SIX

Destruction Corps

FOR A thousand years, Dublin had suffered chronic unemployment and when I left Malin, it hadn't got much better. I couldn't find a job anywhere. Malin prepared you for one of two things: jail or the army. So, pretending to be my brother, I said I was eighteen and joined up. There was a war on and it was three months before they found me out. Then an angry sergeant paraded me before an amused colonel.

'So you are only fourteen years of age.'

'Fourteen years eleven months,' I corrected.

'Well, I'm sorry, you're too young for us. You'll have to go.'

And so I found myself on the loose again. This time I determined to try for the Construction Corps. This was a Hitler Youth idea dreamed-up by de Valera. The principle was simple enough. To solve the problem of the unemployed, call them up: draft all your young men into labour battalions, subject to military discipline but not required to bear arms. Judges gave kids heading for Borstal or prison the option of two years in the corps or six months inside. It was no wonder that some of the recruits were such hard nuts. I became 1599 Behan.

As soon as I joined I could tell that the regular army didn't know what the hell to do with us. The N.C.O.s did their best but the new recruit had to fight for his life from the day he started. My kit vanished the first night I had it. Some bright spark just ignored my heavy duty padlock and chopped the bottom out of the box, using the fire drill hatchet. When I opened it, I was just staring at the bare floor. Here my Malin training held me in good stead. I said nothing but simply toddled along to another room and pinched someone else's. Still the Corps had its advantages. Our food was assured, as were our clothes and bed; and, with its insistence on clean living you kept fit and healthy.

After a few weeks hanging about McKee Barracks, we were sent out on our first job. I found myself on my way to work on the shores of

Loch Ramour, touching the edges of Virginia Village, County Cavan. It was a lovely spot. We were stationed in an old rectory that had six beautiful lawns stretching right down to the lakeside. We lived three to a room and it was home from home. In the morning if you were up early enough you could see hundreds of rabbits drumming their feet on the ground.

The only thing that I had against country life was the scarcity of girls. My one thought when I knew I was leaving Malin and returning to the city was—girls! Girls talking under the street lamps in the evenings, or sitting in the old Sundrive cinema pretending not to notice all the hordes of young fellows climbing over the seats and throwing sweet papers at them. My years of monkdom had put me out of practice, and when I did get in the proximity of a girl I found myself tongue-tied. Then one night in the pictures I met an old friend, Dennis. When we were about six, we planned to buy a rowing boat and go to sea. We even walked all the way to Dollymount to look some over. We had saved sixpence, but the boats were much dearer than we expected, so the partnership broke up. Anyway, Dennis had grown up to be a real lady killer. I think he models his technique on Clark Gable, for he worked to a formula of two smacks a kiss. Under his tutelage, I began to enjoy small successes. I joyfully discovered that girls who had previously fought and kicked in earnest when I pressed them up against the wall with their hands caught behind them—now seemed to lack the strength, and I could put my hands to better use.

But then we got stuck out in the wilds where there seemed to be no girls at all. One day I set out to see the village with my two mates. Our path led us right round strawberry beds at the edge of the lake. We were strolling quite gaily along when we heard some girls call 'Yoo hoo!' The girls were laughing and tittering at us behind some bushes. Interested, we started after them, only to see them run, stark naked, into the lake.

'They're the three jokers I was telling you about,' said my mate, 'three right old pushers.'

'Old!' I exclaimed, 'but one of them only looked about twelve.'

'That's Maggie, she's fourteen, come with us tonight and we might see her again.'

Intrigued by this good news, I went with him to the house dance.

This was simply a dance held in the back room of a single woman's cottage. I soon found Carmel, the middle joker, as my partner. She was sixteen and she had a deep dark fringe. She wasn't terribly pretty, but was soft, fresh and female; and she didn't demur when I suggested we should take a walk outside. In no time at all we were down by the shores of the lake and I was kissing and hugging her to the beat of the band. She made no resistance when I went further and I was just on the point of making real love to her when I heard the bushes move behind me. It was her younger sister Margaret. 'Carmel,' she called, 'come quick, daddy's looking for you.' It might have been a gag, but Carmel jumped up and scurried away, pulling up her knickers as she ran.

The following night I went again to see if I could find her. She was with the crowd hanging round the fish and chipper, but she completely ignored me. I had half lost interest when my mate told me that he had fixed up to go to the next Saturday's dance with all three of them.

Coming home from the dance, we parked ourselves in the village graveyard and started the lovely old hand-fumbling, heart-thudding sport. Suddenly, there was a crashing in the bushes, and bright lights shone all over us. It was the local vigilantes led by the parish priest. These bands of frustrated ladies and gentlemen, pillars of the Church all, would roam the country in a great sweat, seeking out happy sinners. They had been known to beat people up, and I started looking round for a means of escape. However, it was only a Protestant graveyard and they let us go.

Not all the stations were as civilised as that one. Next I was transferred to Glencree, up in the Wicklow Mountains. They chose to send us there on a winter's day when the driving snow almost blinded us in the open back of our army truck. Higher and higher we climbed until we got on a featherbed road. There we rode along as high as the hills on either side. This road was built by British engineers to try to capture Michael Dwyer, the rebel chief who had taken sanctuary in the mountains. We descended into Glencree valley very sharply, and pulled up outside the old reformatory that was to be our barracks.

We were up there to build a road from the valley up to Sally Gap, a distance of about three miles. For three months, January, February and March, we toiled at it carrying the rocks out of the quarry and dropping them on the frost-covered heather foundation. On a clear day, the village was very, very beautiful. In front rose three pins of mountains with the sea at their backs. Beside us was Old Eagle Rock, its bald granite pate eternally looking down on Lough Bray. A long narrow scar gouged out by countless years, the lake is clear, still and wonderful.

Last winter, my wife and I went back to look at it again. We hitch-hiked out on a frosty morning just before Christmas. It was a brilliantly sunny day. The mountain tops were white and the air was magically still and silent. The bog water that runs eternally down the mountains had frozen as it dripped onto the road so that we walked beside a hanging wall of icicles and fairy caves. We left the road and followed the sheep tracks around the boggy mountainside. Above us a startled hare scudded away for dear life, leaving his hunched shape printed for ever on the horizon of my memory. In front of us now, the rill that feeds the lake was caught, trapped in an icy grip; suspended in mid air until the Spring should come to set it free. We found some rocks to rest upon and lay looking down on the still lake dazzling in the sunshine, and, beyond it, the wooded valley. Here I had worked in the warm sweet-smelling pine woods, warm on the coldest winter's day.

The next job after Glencree took us to Coolronan Bog in Westmeath where the land was low and wet. We lived on a farm run by a man and his sister. Miggins, their name was. Jack Miggins was a gentle man of hard work and few words. Once he came with us to a fair at Mullingar. We had a go at throwing the fifty-six pound weight and laughingly pressed Jack to try his luck. He refused at first, but then he casually picked it up and just threw it like a stone farther, by ten feet, than anyone before him.

The bog is really a rotting forest pressed down on the bed of the Irish Plain. Seemingly endless, it stretches flat and bleak for twenty-six miles. On first acquaintance, it looks dead and lifeless, but after a while, especially in the Spring, you'll notice all sorts of things in it: insects, frogs, small fish and birds by the thousand. There's always a lark twittering unseen somewhere above you, or the curlews' eerie cry to give you the shivers and bring to mind tales of people lost on the bog never to be seen again. A bog hole is sometimes bottomless and always black and sinister. I fell into one once and couldn't get out because the sides kept on falling in on me. I started to howl like a prairie dog and was rescued just in time by my sergeant. It is said that the bog will preserve anything. Butter has been left in it for months and retrieved still quite edible. The bog is a good place to hide a body as it closes over and leaves no trace: the only drawback is that it is liable to be still there intact years later. A haunting thought that which puts me off the whole idea.

I've been told that but for the granite bed, the peat bog would have become a huge coalfield. Imagine if it had, and Ireland had become the industrial centre of these islands. No emigration; no Kennedys; no bull-necked Irish police chiefs denying rights that their grandsires had been denied in Ireland, and had sought and found in America.

I started gambling while working on the bog and lost my wages week after week. One night I was serving supper in the cook-house when a rowdy crowd came in demanding quick service. I was in a murderous mood having once again lost all my wages. So I promptly gave the first of them quick service in the shape of a bang on the head with a dixie full of mashed potatoes. They challenged me to come out from behind the counter. Still in a rage, I leapt over and as quick as a flash two of them grabbed my arms while a third punched my guts in for me. I thought it was goodnight but the provost sergeant heard the noise and came in and saved me. However, I didn't learn my lesson, for soon after that I got into a poker school and saw two pokers out at one time. There were four kings and four aces and I had bad luck to have three nines. Towards the end of the game, I and another man did a 'Hula hula' on the pool. We just started to shout: 'Sergeant's coming!' and in the confusion grabbed the money and made off with it. A shameful thing to do no doubt, but then gambling makes people do shameful things.

Long before the end of my two years' service, I was sick to death with the corps. The novelty of an assured three meals a day soon palls and seems a poor exchange for freedom. So I was very glad indeed when my time was up and I passed through the gates of McKee Barracks for the very last time.

CHAPTER SEVEN

Brotherly Love

MY FIRST job was under a foreman named Ned Mullholland. On a cold summer morning I waited outside his house on a new estate. Like Ned, the house was spotless. A house where no children interrupted the flow of carbolic soap and Brasso. There was only his sister, and she had given up dolls twenty years before. He talked as we made our way to the job. 'So you're Stephen Behan's boy. Well you'll be all right with me. Yes I'm a bit of a communist meself you know.' I looked at him in surprise. 'Ah, that shook you, didn't it? Yes, I'm a red; a Catholic of course. I go to mass and devotions, but still I believe in every man getting a fair crack of the whip.'

I felt the tension that had been twisting at my insides at the thought of a new job gradually ease. To start a new job at any time was bad enough; to start as a navvy at the age of sixteen was murder, especially as I now supported the Communists which put me in violent opposition to ninety-nine-point-nine per cent of my fellow men. Since a child I had known that the bosses were our enemy. And to me, my enemy's enemies must be my friends. It never entered my head that they might just be peas in a pod.

My father had been a trade unionist all his life. Dublin was a 'no ticket, no start' town for building tradesmen. On a Saturday after my mother had finished shopping in Moore Street, she would say, 'Come on and we'll all pay your father's hall money.' The hall was in Aungier Street, a gloomy hole in which men just stood around. In front was the 'buck cat' who sat at his little table taking in money. In 1936, we starved for seven months during one of the longest strikes the trade had seen. We were so far gone that one day we boiled up mother's old pin-cushion and ate the oatmeal out of it, full though it was of years of fluff and dirt. My mother was a natural anarchist: she didn't need any organisation to fight for her. She could fight her way out of a barrel full of tigers. A baker once sold me a loaf that was rock hard. It was

our last tanner and mother went back with it. After some humming
and hawing, he refused to take it back, so, in a fury, she belted him
right across the nose with it.

Our job was building an estate of bungalows for the respectable,
middle-class man. From his back garden he was to look out onto the
rising slopes of the Dublin hills; from the front, he would have a clear
view to the sparkling sea, dancing and shining around the Hill of
Howth. Not that I had much time to enjoy the view. Ned, true to his
beliefs, was making sure that I got that fair crack of the whip—right
across my back. All day long he hounded me. To make it worse, he
hadn't the faintest notion of what a good day's work was—for a navvy.
A joiner by trade, he spent all his life in the shop, and this was his first
attempt at foreman on an open site. He put me to digging a trench with
Chris Tobin. Tobin was a man of about fifty. Hard as oak, he remained single in an attempt to avoid the back-breaking burden of a
married man. 'Why keep a cow when you can buy a pint of milk?' was
his motto. Even so, he wasn't happy. In front of him was Paddy
Neville, a big, powerfully-built, round-shouldered boxer. He too was
unmarried but not yet old enough to have become crabby for want of
children and a home.

The stuff we were digging was yellow marl: a sticky, gluey clay.
You get it about ten feet down, near hills. To dig it was like trying to empty the ocean with a teaspoon. It sticks to your shovel and
traps your feet. Tobin had made himself a little raft to stand on,
and went up and down digging a bit at a time dipping his shovel
into a bucket of water every few throws so that the marl would
slip off as he threw it up the bank. At my first attempt, lacking
both bucket and raft, I nearly tore myself in two. The lump of
marl remained where it was on the shovel and I would have
flown up with it only my feet had sunk a foot down preventing
me from taking off. I tried to keep up with the others but it nearly
killed me. By evening, my hands were red-raw from sliding up and
down the thick shovel handle. Next day they were covered in blisters
as soon as I tried to work, they burst and my hands were soon raw
and bleeding.

A thousand times I cursed Ned. I prayed that the hairs on his head
might turn into club hammers and beat his stinking brains out. I had

sweet visions of tossing him into the concrete mixer and watching the blades chew him up. And yet I never thought of packing the job up. I suppose it was because jobs were hard to get and every man's first question was 'Working?' The thought of actually giving the job up was sacrilegious.

I wasn't alone in my hatred for Ned. Neville and Tobin called him a bloody, craw-thumping hypocrite. It was true, he was a religious maniac. He would never curse or indulge in sexy talk. For a while, he took to blessing the men; from under his coat he would whip out a bottle of holy water and, pretending to sprinkle us, would make the sign of the cross. Being lowly labourers, there was nothing we could do. But one day, Jimmy, a bricklayer, threatened to chop off his hand with a trowel, and that seemed to discourage him for a time.

Apart from dinner-hour, the only time to escape from Ned was at lavatory time. With a view to discouraging idleness, Ned had built a lavatory of the most rudimentary design. He simply had us hollow out a trench six foot deep and three wide. Over this, he had suspended a wooden scaffold pole nailed to three uprights. Around this temple he had placed a screen made up of sheets of galvanised tin. Apart from the fact that there was no privacy, it was the feat of a Houdini to be able to get astride that greasy pole on a wet and windy day.

With the passage of time, the trench was now filled to overflowing.

Now for some time, Ned had been needling Neville: perhaps he hated his calm, unhurried way of working. Whatever the reason, he wouldn't leave him alone. One dinner-hour, Neville was just recounting a particularly filthy tale when he turned to find Ned glaring at him. 'You should keep your dirty tongue to yourself, Neville,' he said, 'instead of infecting this young boy with your germs.' Neville said nothing but only flushed as red as a beetroot.

It was the custom on the job for everyone to sing the praises of the guvnor, Brady. The loudest voice in the chorus was always that of foreman Ned. He even told me that the overtime we did was a special concession from Mr Brady to help married men. One dinner-hour as we sat outside munching our sandwiches, a telegraph boy came rolling up on his bicycle and handed Ned a telegram. 'Any reply, sir?' Ned shook his head and stood there bemused. For about an hour he went about his business humming and talking to himself. Later in the afternoon a car drew up and out stepped Mr Brady himself. Smiling as happily as a pig in muck, Tobin ran forward and tried to beam his servility onto his master, but Brady took about as much notice as a bull treading upon an ant. Ned, as a rule, would hear Brady's car two miles away, and would be waiting at the gate to make obeisance, but today he was nowhere to be seen.

Brady snorted angrily. 'Where's Ned?' he barked.

'I'm up here,' called Ned, grinning like a Cheshire cat.

'Well come down here!' shouted Brady. 'I can't talk while you're hanging round like a monkey in a bloody zoo.'

With a crazy whoop, Ned jumped gleefully down into a pile of sand.

Astonished, Brady pushed back his kingfisher hat and scratched his head. 'What on earth has got into you, Mullholland?'

'Nothing, nothing at all; I was only thinking to meself.'

'Well I'm damn sure it wasn't about your work you were thinking. What's the idea of refusing to accept deliveries of cement?'

'I hadn't the room; the sheds are full already.'

'You could have made room. My God, man, don't you know there's going to be a cement strike? Or can't you read? Are you trying to ruin me, or what? Do you think I had it sent out here for fun. I'm afraid if you carry on like this you won't be working for me much longer.'

'Well, you could be right at that,' said Ned.

'What are you getting at?'

Standing with his hands behind his back like Napoleon, Ned gave forth. 'I'm not getting at anything. I am telling you that I'm finished. Finished working for you or anyone else.' He waved the bit of paper aloft and screamed 'I've won the Sweep! Oh yes, I don't have to stay here timber-butchering another moment. All my family before me were real joiners and cabinet-makers, not woodchoppers. Now I'll be back again in me own shop, me own master.'

At once, Brady's manner changed. Sticking out his paw, he congratulated Ned. 'Well, Ned, no one is more happy than me to hear it. I wish you all you wish yourself. No hard feeling now.'

Ned was all puffed, like a toad. 'Oh that's all right,' he condescended, 'anyone can have a row now and again.'

He packed his tools and pulled out that night.

I, speechless with jealousy, was cursing the fates that would smile money down on a dried-up old cod who wouldn't know what to do with it—while I was wasting my talents down a muddy trench.

'Fancy spending it on a lousy joiner's shop,' I moaned to Neville.

'Sure he'll get no joiner's shop, lad, you needn't worry about that.'

'What do you mean?'

'Well, it's all a joke, see. We put the telegraph boy up to it. He's Tobin's nephew. Ned never won anything at all.'

All my feelings made a rapid reverse. 'What a lousy, rotten thing to do.'

I went for Neville then. I felt like killing him. Poor little me. He just drew out and put me on the broad of my back.

The last I heard of Ned was a rumour that he had gone religious mad. He was clear out of his mind and in some home wandering the never-ending circle and giggling to himself.

A new foreman appeared on the job, and though he didn't profess any communist leanings, he also held fast to the 'fair crack of the whip' theory. My hands were hard by now, but other, bigger men were begging every day for work on the site, and I didn't last long.

CHAPTER EIGHT

On the Dole

MY EARLY unemployed days were happy ones. I had only myself to keep, and the mountains and sea were there on my doorstep, and at last I really had the time to enjoy them. True, we sometimes had bread and marge to take with us, but when you've been swimming or hiking all day, bread, even bread and marge, can be delicious. Out of the twenty-two-and-six dole money, I used to give my mother a pound and keep the half crown for a trip to the pictures and five Woodbines. To get the dole you had to sign on three days a week. Sometimes the long lines of unemployed would spill out and stretch right away down the street. From time to time you would hear of a man or woman who had died of slow starvation. I asked our local parish priest why he didn't denounce the evils of capitalism as vigorously as he denounced those of Communism far away. He told me that the Church never interfered in politics.

Our family had always been a political one. My father had spent time in jail for his I.R.A. activities and was a leading member of his union, but the first smell of Marxism came from my brother Sean. He got the bug very badly and joined the Irish Workers' League which was really the old Communist Party revived under a more innocuous name. For my own part, I had always contested the right of any party to control my actions and to force me to carry out decisions with which I did not agree. I believed then as I do now that a man must finally be true to his own conscience and follow the dictates of his own experience. The greatest of saints and humanists can founder and do terrible harm once they relinquish this right. My whole life has been a search for an organisation that would bring happiness to humanity, only to find that all organisations become an end in themselves, thriving on, and perpetuating, human misery and backwardness. As far as I'm concerned, any organisation of more than one person (except one man and one woman) is suspect.

About the time Sean joined the Communists I began to use my spare time in organising a youth movement. Many of the people in the dole-queue were youngsters and we were all stirred up not only at being unemployed but also because a number of kids had recently drowned swimming in the gravel pits. We began to campaign for a swimming pool for Crumlin, and out of this grew the Democratic Youth Movement. It had an astonishing success. Within a month we had a membership of over a hundred and a magazine selling two thousand copies. We were suppressed eventually by a combination of the Church on our right hand and the Irish Workers' League on our left. The Church attacked us through pamphlets in which they accused us of violating the Blessed Virgin at our meetings. This incited the local fanatics against us and frightened young people away. But the death blow was struck by the orthodox Marxists. Unfortunately, I and a few of the youth movement leaders had fallen for the old jargon and joined them. And now they had the wind up because they feared that the youth movement was supplanting them, and crime of crimes, we, with our empirical and free approach, weren't always on the party line. This could not be tolerated. The British C.P. sent over their regular Irishman, Desmond Greaves, for the purpose of brainwashing me, and after much heart-searching, we agreed to a merger. Inside two weeks the youth movement disintegrated.

I had long been puzzling my head to find a way to organise the unemployed to fight for better conditions. One day in the queue I met a man called Johnny Byrne. He was just over from Liverpool and had been active in the C.P. there. He had a refreshingly honest and practical approach—that is, he wasn't addicted to long theoretical discussions—and he suggested that we should start a controversy in the letter-columns of the Dublin *Evening Mail*. This we did, and it wasn't long before we had a thriving movement going. One day I was on my way to the Labour Exchange when a crudely written notice hanging from the railings attracted my attention. It said, 'I, Sean Hynes, announce my intention of going on hunger strike on O'Connell Bridge at nine o'clock this Friday morning.' And in smaller letters underneath—'against the persecution of the Irish Catholic unemployed.'

With a bit of searching I found him. He was living in a new council house on the outskirts of the city. A very ordinary-looking man he was, short and thin with a brush-like moustache.

'Are you serious about this hunger strike?' I asked him.

'I was never more serious about anything,' he replied. 'I might as well starve to death in the open as do it in here.'

Sitting round him were his wife and a couple of kids, one of them a baby in a pram. His wife nodded agreement and said, 'I am behind Sean to the hilt, come what may.'

He had been a statue-maker and had been paid off to make way for cheaper labour fleeing from Communist tyranny. For a while he had eked out his dole money making little Blessed Childs of Prague for his neighbours. He showed me his rows of Blessed Virgin Marys, all too dear for his neighbours' pockets. Twelve months of semi-starvation had driven him to this desperate step. I was getting up to go when a knock came at the door. One of his young fellas came running in shouting, 'Daddy, Daddy there's a big car at the door.'

On the doorstep stood a neatly dressed young priest.

'Mr Hynes?' he asked.

Hynes nodded. As he went to speak Hynes stopped him.

'Come on inside Father, there's no sense in filling up the neighbours' mouths.'

The priest hesitated, 'No, no, Mr Hynes, it's all right, what I have to say won't take a minute.'

Hynes just turned and began to walk away saying, 'Stop where you are then, if my kitchen is not good enough for you.'

Discomforted, the priest had no option but to follow. As soon as he got into the kitchen he smiled.

'What I had to say Mr Hynes was private.'

'I have no secrets from my wife and family, we are all in this together,' said Hynes, looking straight at him.

'Well,' began the priest, 'I have a message for you from the Archbishop.'

'Oh,' said Hynes. 'I hope it's better news than was in his letter.'

'Oh, come now Mr Hynes, his Grace is a busy man, his job is a difficult one.'

'Well, you can tell the Archbishop I would swop jobs with him any day of the week. Let him try feeding my six kids on thirty-eight shillings a week and see how he likes it.'

'Come, Mr Hynes, I am surprised to hear you, a good Catholic, talking like that. I can assure you that you are in his Grace's thoughts and while he can't assist you in getting a job he sends you this.'

He placed three pound notes on the table. From where I was sitting I could see Mrs Hynes look longingly at the money. Hynes just picked it up and handed it back to the priest.

'It's too late for that now, Father. It's funny how everyone wants to give me charity now, but I am not a beggar. I didn't start this thing to get money, I want a job that will enable me to keep my wife and children, and I'm going on hunger strike till I get one.'

As the priest stood up he made a final appeal. 'I must warn you that what you are doing is a mortal sin, the Church will not take kindly to a suicide.'

It was Hynes' wife who answered him. 'No, Father, we aren't committing suicide, we are being starved to death inside these four walls and no one cares because they can't see us. Well, they're going to see Sean tomorrow.'

I made arrangements to meet Hynes the following morning to give him what help I could. His problem, really, was to get on the bridge before the police grabbed him. My plan was to wait until Hynes was ready to start from one end and then to cause a diversion at the other. Nine o'clock came and the bridge was alive with police. A fly couldn't have rested on it, let alone Hynes. Then I saw Hynes get off a bus and make slowly for the far end of the bridge. Quick as a flash, I jumped up on to a box and started to roar—'People of Dublin, will you let Hynes starve to death?' My roar nearly frightened the wits out of a double-deck bus driver who braked like a lunatic thinking the hour of judgment was at hand. The police, hearing my shout, thought Hynes was with me and all made a concerted drive for our platform. I was hauled down double quick. A mate of mine, John Byrne, jumped up after me. He was pulled down. In the meantime, Hynes, draped fore and aft in big posters, made his way to the middle of the bridge. The press were around him like wasps round a pot of jam. Taking snaps, asking questions, the lot. Eventually, the police had him away too. We were told to clear off or they'd run us in.

In court later, the judge was lecturing Hynes.

'You must know, my man, the disgrace you are bringing on this whole city by your conduct. Don't you care what worry you cause your poor wife.'

Leaning forward, Hynes spoke up. 'Your Honour, my wife is with me in this. If there is any disgrace it lies on those who let us starve.'

The Justice seemed to get angry.

'Now see here, my good man, there is no one starving in this city. That is a slander on the people that are working hard in the various charities.'

'I don't want charity, your honour, I want a job, I have written everywhere, even to the Archbishop, I have his letter here.'

Before the Judge could stop him Hynes was away reading the letter: ' "Dear Mr Hynes, I am deeply aware of your predicament, how-ever, there is simply nothing I can do. We have numerous calls that we can only refer to the charitable organisations. Yours in Christ, John McQuaid." '

I thought the old judge would have a fit. 'I have heard enough, Hynes, I will bind you over to keep the peace and fine you one shilling in default of which you will go to prison for one month.'

'I won't pay it,' called up Hynes.

The Judge pondered and then he said rather testily, 'Oh, very well, if you can't pay it then I will arrange for it to be paid out of the court poor box.'

Hynes gripped the front of the box and shouted up, 'I didn't say I couldn't pay the shilling, I said I wouldn't pay it.'

At this, the crowd burst out cheering and started to roar and stamp their feet. I saw Hynes for a couple of minutes before they took him away to do the month. He seemed in good spirits.

'Brian, tell my wife I'm still on hunger strike, I will go through with this now.'

That night, we spoke to one of the biggest meetings Dublin has ever seen. The whole city had heard about Hynes, the ordinary little man with the heart of a lion. The meeting ended peacefully enough but a feeling of tension and expectancy hung in the air.

A Labour councillor, Barney Conway (an old comrade of Jim

Larkin), got us in to see Hynes. It was his seventh day and he looked as fresh as a daisy.

'Ah well,' he laughed, 'I have plenty of training for this job you might say.'

He told us not to look so gloomy, he would beat them yet.

'Look,' he expounded. 'I never told you that I once did two years in here as a warder. I know that when a man goes on hunger strike the whole prison is placed on the alert. All leave is cancelled and the Governor has no option but to be here twenty-four hours a day. Can you imagine the state they would be in if a couple of hundred of you fellas got yourselves arrested and immediately all went on hunger strike. We would paralyse them.'

In the middle of the second week the Government collapsed. They threw Hynes out of prison and got him a permanent job. Despite this, he still used to come to our unemployed meetings, and clutching his bicycle pump, regaled us with tales of doctors whom he swore 'were practising on the children of the poor.'

Shortly after that I got a start as a carter. I had very little knowledge of horses, particularly great big ones. I soon found that the company expected every horse to earn his keep. Our main job was shifting stuff from the docks to the city merchants' stores. I started on timber with a half-cut horse called Oak. Then I tried Portuguese slates and wound up drawing oil in quarter-ton barrels for Castrols. I have always loved children, but now they nearly killed me. I was driving along over Baggott Street Bridge when a barrel of oil flew by me and struck Oak a glancing blow across the rump. Old Oak saved my life. A younger horse would have dashed down the hill pulling the other nine barrels on top of me. Slowly, I edged him into the path, steadying the next barrel as it rocked on its wedge. Some kids I had given a lift to earlier on had whipped one of the wedges from under the front of the barrel.

To my annoyance one morning I found myself locked out of the yard. A picket marched up and down. It was the first and last time I was in a strike without having any hand or part in starting it. From what I could gather, the strike was over the sacking of a shop steward at one of the other depots. For weeks the dispute dragged on, crippling the pockets of married men. I stood up at one meeting and asked if the strike was a serious one why didn't the union call out the rest of the transport workers? There was no reply. Then in the fifth week our union started putting up posters attacking the other transport union, which was British based. 'Irish men join an Irish Union,' proclaimed our leaflets. Men who were in the other union were treated with much more hostility than our Superintendent. After six weeks we went back to work. The only thing gained by our union was a 100 per cent monopoly of organisation, the other union having pulled out. What gain that was I'll never know. I, like all the others, still had to slog my guts out for £5 7s. 6d. per week.

Because I spoke up during the strike arguing for either an extension of the strike or its ending I found myself hedged in between the yard supervisor and the union's delegate. Very soon I found I was being hired less and less. Being casual labour we worked on a day-to-day basis. Within a couple of weeks I found myself getting four, two, and then one day's work. Finally I was back on the dole.

CHAPTER NINE

Tramp, Tramp, Tramp

THE IRISH Government hit upon another device for clearing the Labour Exchanges. As you presented your body to register as unemployed, the hatch-clerk asked, 'Do you want a job?'

If you said no you were automatically disqualified from receiving any more dole. So after you recovered from the shock, you fearfully said 'Of course.' In Dublin, the hatch-clerks are protected from their clients by high wire nets. As fast as you answered yes the dirty swine were issuing out travel vouchers to take you to the Turf Camps. The powers that be were trying to kill two birds with one stone. Develop the peat industry by pouring the unemployed out onto the vast plains of the Bog of Allen.

My first day didn't begin too well. Our long lean country bus stopped for a quarter of an hour outside a pub in a remote village. Inside, I fell in with some tinkers who treated me right royally and well. Too well in fact—I emerged from the pub to see my bus vanishing down the road with my bag and baggage on top.

Tinkers are by nature very quarrelsome people, and, what's more, they believe in sharing their troubles. My tinkers had the usual yellow scarf knotted round their necks and wore great big hats. Their women wore shawls draped around their shoulders and their long, dirty, black hair hung down their backs. Very soon they began staggering round in the half-light of the pub. The front of the pub was a shop, and the little publican didn't take too kindly to the tinkers trying to induce his women customers into the back. As we drank on, the tinkers started to chide one another about various things. Women and horses seemed the main bones of discontent. Suddenly, one of them flourished a long-handled whip and challenged another to fight with whips. In a second the little publican was round the bar appealing to the two men. 'In the name of God, don't wreck the place.' Without a word, the two tinkers marched out the door and stood opposite each other. I had a feeling that the two of them would have liked to have called it off but the crowd that had gathered egged them on to fight like dogs. At first it seemed more like a propaganda war than anything else. There were no blows struck for the first five minutes. All you could hear was a stream of abuse streaming back and forth between the two. One of them was a young fair-haired man of about twenty-five. The other was middle-aged and as black as the Earl of Hell's waistcoat. The women had ceased their general screeching and one, the wife of the black-haired one, started to taunt her man.

'Are you going to let him get away with calling your wife a whore —ah, my God, it's not blood that passes through your veins, it's water.' Pushing him forward, she shouted 'Are you going to teach that black-guard a lesson, or will I have to fight him meself?'

Half stumbling, half falling, the black tinker made a run at blondy. They wrestled and heaved for a while until blondy fell flat on his back with the black one on top of him.

At this the crowd began to titter and laugh. 'He loves him,' called one. 'No, it's a new kind of dancing!' cried another. Kneeling on top of the other man, blacky began to pound away at him beating him across the mouth. All that the young man could do was to put his two arms over his face to protect himself.

Laughing and grinning, the black devil rained blow upon blow down on top of him shouting 'I'll beat manners into you even if your old mother didn't.' I looked round for help, convinced that murder would be done if I didn't. But all I could see was the lone village policeman beating a hasty retreat. It was the black tinker's wife, the cause of the dispute, who rushed to catch his arm. This seemed to en-rage him even more. Catching her by the throat, he shouted 'You dirty bitch, so you want to help your fancy man, well I'll leave him so that he won't be able to run after another man's wife.' As they wrestled to and fro, she suddenly broke away. Inflamed with drink, she reached up and tore the whole front of her dress right down, displaying her two pear-shaped breasts.

Slapping her belly, she turned on the crowd and declaimed 'You're a born liar, Mike McCarthy, I never lay under any man except you. There's a belly that never bore a bastard.'

Rushing at her, he started wrestling with her again. Catching her by the neck, he drew back his fist to punch her.

At this, I rushed in and started to belt him in the guts. I might have managed him but I felt a terrible bang on the back of my skull. I pitched forward on my knees and heard his wife shout:

'Leave my poor husband alone, you murdering bastard. The cheek of ye coming between man and wife.'

The camp that I eventually got to seemed a decent enough place, rows of neat concrete huts with a wide green space in the middle. Each camp had a commandant, army style. Ours wore a uniform of his own design. He began with heavy brogue shoes and khaki gaiters under brown plus-fours. With his deerstalker hat and tweedy jacket, he looked a cross between a country squire and Sherlock Holmes.

The grub was a mixture. The breakfast seemed fair enough. You had a bit of a fry and then a whole loaf with some meat and butter on top of it. Surprised at the seeming generosity of the Board, I said to a big Aran Island man, 'I don't think I would ever eat all that at one session.'

'Don't worry,' he answered me, 'you won't have to eat it all now; that loaf is supposed to do you till six o'clock tonight.'

That night we travelled back in kraaled wagons like cattle. The wind whipped the turf mould up off the floor of the lorry, blinding and blackening us. Tired and weary, we staggered into dinner. Dinner! Whoever named it that was joking: potatoes half raw and meat so small that you wouldn't feed a cat on it. To discourage the men from packing the job in, the Board never allowed you to get a lift in their wagons back to the main base for pay. This meant that if you left you had to walk all of fifteen miles. About three weeks later, I was doing that walk.

I had to pull out. I could smell trouble a mile off. In the first place, our pay was so little that it sometimes amounted to two shillings a week. The fiddle worked in this way. Your basic time rate was supposed to be eightpence an hour plus your board and lodgings. But all operations from the day you started were at piece rates. Because the measurements were in metres it was extremely hard to follow the ganger's calculations. So nine cases out of ten, he simply booked your work down to someone else. Of course they sometimes suffered from this.

One ganger had been soundly beaten up three times in as many weeks. Even by dint of half killing yourself, you could earn up to only ten or twelve shillings a week. The result was that the place was more like a transit camp than anything else—men coming and going all day long.

Again, in some bogs, you get a thing known as 'wig.' This is a long hard strand of stuff that defies cutting no matter how strong the cutter. As it runs right up through the bank, it can prevent the cutter earning anything at all day after day. Despite all this, our commandant still wanted to play a cheerful chappie. He would regularly address the men in the canteen urging them to support the Board's paper, *An Slean*. One night after the men had eaten a particularly vile pudding, he answered their complaints by eating a little and saying 'I like it very much' . . . The men started to bang their mugs on the tables all together. He still tried to make himself heard but it was a dead loss; they just drowned him out. Then just as quickly as it began, it stopped. Relieved, he started to look round hoping to detect some change in the expressions on the men's faces. There was none.

(Down on the bog, men went, what they called, dog-rough. They let their hair grow until they looked like divine apostles with the ends growing curly back up their necks. Most of them had abandoned shaving. They had no need to shave. No one lived on the bog. All that you had round it were scattered cottages. When the Board held a dance if two women turned up it was as much as could be hoped for. The men simply buck-danced in their boots like the Klondike miners.)

Our commandant was a silly man. Instead of getting out of it, he started off again. 'I tell you, men, I have tasted the sweet and I think it's substantial, I repeat, I quite liked it.'

A stout, bearded Kerry man decided to play the fool. 'You quite liked it then, sir,' he called.

'Why yes, Donnelly, I did.'

'Then you can have mine,' he said, and flung his bowl right at him.

This became the signal for hundreds of bowls to fly amidst a general chorus of 'No, have mine, sir.' 'Don't have his, have mine.'

Only poor shooting, combined with bowls hitting each other in the air, saved the commandant from serious injury. Even so, he was splattered from head to toe with thick grey slime. That night I decided to bail out. Despite a strike that had lasted for three weeks, nothing had improved. They just left the men to starve. When they marched to Dublin to show their wounds to the Jackeens, they got scant sympathy. The year I left, the men, feeling all else was useless, poured out of the camps in their thousands.

With no dole and no job there seemed no alternative now to becoming a tramp. A tramp in England can live. He is well provided for in spikes that span the country from one end to the other. Not so in Ireland. The spikes are few and far between. What there are, like the Black Lane shelter or the Morning Star in Dublin, are very dodgy, both requiring extensive work to be performed before breakfast.

There were four of us who started off tramping. That in itself was a bad thing as four will certainly take more feeding than one. There were two of us Dublin men, one from Cork and a man from Wexford called Power whom I suspected was a tinker once removed. The Cork man was tall and stout. An imposing man, he could sing like a bird. He was useless at working though: all his energy went into making people laugh. From our very first day out, I had a feeling it was no good. We walked through Newbridge and out onto the Plains to the Curragh Camp just as the red sun was setting over Monasterevan. Up a gently sloping hill we went, all round us the miles of grass that once fed the remounts for the Indian army. From here had gone the ponies to play polo in the mountains of Northern India. From here my grandfather had packed his possessions and set out to man the Khyber Pass. There he reared another family. I love to think that little Indian Behans are dotting the plains below Japutte. As we tramped along, we became footsore and weary. I had never in my life been so totally lacking in food and shelter. The food I could do without but the thought of a nice warm bed fairly thrilled me through and through. Then away in the gathering dusk, I saw the lights of a bus. I turned to the rest and said 'Here, look, let's get this bus back to town, we can be indoors by ten o'clock.'

I knew that, despite my mother's disappointment at seeing me again without money and job, I could still rest there for a while. Though of late things had been difficult at home. My mother didn't let idlers rest peacefully in their beds. Her constant stream of propaganda would have put Goebbels to shame. 'Are you content to see

your father kill himself while you eat idle bread?' Then, 'Your poor
father was coughing again last night. Will you drive him to his grave a
poor white-haired old man before his time?' And 'May the good God
forgive you, for I'm sure I never will, for what you expect that poor
man to do.' Or 'Surely there must be some job you can get or are you
content to lose the use of your limbs from all this lying in that bed.' But
how could you blame my mother. Was my father doomed to keep
grown men who only used his house to hold meetings in?

Even so, I was delighted to see the bus roll up like a fairy coach. It
stopped for us all right, but, alas and alack, it was empty returning not
to Dublin but to Kildare garage not half a mile away. Sadly, we walked
on.

I found the Irish countryman to be a mixture. Smiling 'God save
you there,' in the daytime, while at night he barricaded himself in like
a feudal lord awaiting siege. We could find nowhere, and had to make
good with a rat-infested barn. The only hay we could find was old and
rotten and, as it was at the top of a haycart, we had to sleep almost
standing as the cart tipped if we tried lying flat. We had to get out of it
early as the peasants came rooting round in the dawn with very
healthy-looking dogs. Our next night we spent in a field that bordered
a railway line. As we pulled the hay over us and lay back, we could see
in the distance the sparks thrown off by an engine. Then it started to
wail, and I thought I would cry for sadness seeing that great warm
trunk slide cheerfully by. I wanted to stop it, to shout out 'Hey there!
I am lying here cold and miserable.' And cold I was; I have never felt
so cold before or since. It was my knees I couldn't warm. Thin and
bony, they kept projecting into the frost-charged air. My poor feet
were roaring hot and ached from scraping the heels of my boots. Thankfully I slipped the boots off and let my feet dangle in the cold, wet,
short stubble that lies under hay. When I came to put them on in the
morning I found that I couldn't. Either my feet had swollen or my
boots had shrunk.

Sitting there on the rock-hard ground, I thought of the poets who
had wished for nothing better than the earth for a pillow and the stars
overhead. I almost cried in temper when thinking how I could have
cheerfully strangled the idiot singers who sang about the joys of life and
the open road. It was a misty morning and from the other side of the

hedge I could hear cattle drovers making the ten-mile push to the local fair with their beasts. In front and above, the breath of the cattle formed a little hot cloud that warmed the morning air.

On the third night we tried to crawl into a ditch to sleep but found it occupied by slugs and bugs too noxious to endure. Then glory, glory, I found an old copy of the *Irish Press*. Under situations vacant it carried an advertisement that said: 'Stone-cutters wanted; 1s. 10½d. an hour. Apply Templemore.'

Templemore was a town in North Tipperary not ten miles from where we were. Joyfully I asked the others 'Surely we can bash stones about for one-and-tenpence an hour? All of us have done some work in a quarry.'

The next afternoon we pulled into Templemore. It's a sleepy little town where once upon a time it is said that they had a statue of Christ that bled real blood. When I looked round its vast square and low houses I didn't wonder what they would believe. It was hot and dusty. In the middle of town, at the weighing platform, three locals stood and looked at nothing. Beside them a one-legged man stood, his head swinging round like a sparrow's. As soon as he saw us he came hopping over.

'Good day, lads.'

Anxious to meet anybody who could help us, we responded warmly. 'Yes, it's a fine day, thank God.'

His face was thin and lined like a man that had suffered much. 'Where are you lads heading for?' he asked.

'Why, here,' answered Corky.

He laughed derisively at us. 'Ah, you're joking, sure, no one ever comes to this poxy hole.'

'Well, we have.'

'Then you're crackers, sure, there's nothing here for anybody. Look, if I had the use of my two legs, I'd be gone out of here like a shot.' He stabbed his crutch down the street. 'Look down there, nothing but public houses; all that ever come in here is a few farmers to spend their half-crown and then away out again. I was in Dunkirk, you know.' Noting our surprise, he went on: 'Oh yes, I was with the Irish Guards in the retreat. My officer, a London man, God rest his soul, told me "Mick," he says, "for God's sake, cut and run out of here, our day is done." The poor fella was killed the day after. I left one o' me legs there.'

To change the conversation, I said 'What are those hills up there?' Rising up from the back of the town was a long line of hills that stretched for miles.

'Ah, that's the Devil's Bit. If you go up there and stand in the Gap on a clear day you can see the mouth of the River Shannon running into the Atlantic.'

'I say,' said Corky, 'isn't the Monastery of Mount Mellery near there?'

'Begob, you're right, not too far away.'

'Did you know it at all?'

'Yes I did, as a matter of fact, a very funny thing happened to me there.' We all sat down and looked at him. He had the floor as usual. 'Well, I went there once for a cure after the drink. You know how they offer hospitality to all and sundry: for a week, anyway. Well, I was stuck in a hut with an old buck, and the old man was as mad as a hatter. Even the monks prayed that he might fall down a well or something. Being religious mad, he used to wrap chains around himself. Dirty great cold things they were too. Because he had great gaps of flesh left unbound, he took to wearing an old hair shirt made up of army blankets.'

At this we started tittering.

'Ah no, lads, fair play now, it's God's truth, I tell you. He even tried to dress me up like this. Well every night he would rise at about three and shake me to go out to pray with him. I choked him off, but it was no good, he still kept at it. "Corky," he said, "some day you'll get the call and you'll rise out of that bed to meet your God like the best of us." Howandever, he kept at it, trying to wrap these damn chains round me. One night, the monks gave us a great feed of veal, but God it was savage on the stomach though. I was in and out of the lavatory all day. Well, lads, I lay down to rest when at about three in the morning I got the most ferocious pains. "By heavens," I said to myself, "I must get to the lavatory, and quick about it." Well this old fool, seeing me jump up, reared up himself and started to tie these fuckin' chains round me again. "Corky," he shouts, "you have heard the call, and good man yourself, you're answering to it." I tried to get away

from him as easy as I could, but it was no go. He hung round me like a
serpent. Well, what with my pains and his screeching, I lost all control.
I twisted these chains around his neck and told him: "If you don't
let go of me this very minute, I'll send you to your maker right now."
Still he wouldn't give me rest and kept on about how glad he was to
see the call moving me. In the finish I had to lift him up and tie him
to the rafters by his chains. I had to leave the next day, anyway, so I
never saw him again.'

When we had all finished laughing, I asked the one-legged man the
way to the address in the *Press*. Mystified, he pointed it out down the
street that led to Templemore Railway Station. As the leader, I made
my way up the lane that led to the yard.

The foreman was seated in a small office just at the entrance to the
lane. A broad man, he was dressed in a bib and brace overall with a
clean-looking ruler sticking out of his top pocket.

After brushing the dust off my coat, I extended the *Irish Press* to
him and said, 'Is this your advertisement, then?'

'Why yes, lad, it is, don't tell me you're a stone-cutter.'

'I am, and what's more, I have three more better than myself with
me.'

Pulling his pencil out, he started to poke his chin in and out with it.
'Do you tell me that now; well, that's good news, I must say, but tell
me, where are your tools?'

'Tools? What tools? I don't see much need for many tools to smash
some rocks up. Surely you don't expect us to carry sledgehammers
around in our pockets.'

'Now, now, boy, I think we are getting at cross purposes. I don't
want any stones smashed with sledgehammers, let's get that clear from
the start.'

'But you advertised for stone cutters?'

'Well, so I did, and if you're a stone cutter, the job is yours, and
right welcome you will be. But hold on a minute, come and see if you
can do this class of work.'

He led me up the lane and round a corner. There, stacked in rows,
stood waiting angels and line after line of crosses. Behind them stood
doves in flight over small, delicately-cut cherubs. The foreman smiled,
and waving his hand said 'Are you able to tackle this sort of cutting,

son?' Looking at me kindly, he went on 'Well, I thought not, but I wish ye luck, me old son.'

Crestfallen, I reported back to my followers that we had no job. Slowly, we made our way to the centre of town. Desperate, we lay down outside the police station, hoping to provoke the police into arresting us. At least, then they would have to feed us. No such luck. The station sergeant was as nice as pie and put us on to a man whom he thought might want some work done. Our man was called Ryan, but seeing that the town is all either Ryans or Myers, that's neither here nor there. The job that he wanted us to do was the same that we had marched fifty miles to escape from—turf cutting. He had a bank of turf out on the bog near Liss Duff. To cut this he would pay six pounds between the four of us. By now we had been on the road for four days and our bellies thought our throats were cut, we were so hungry. A big farmer told us he could neither feed nor shelter us. He had oats in his barn and we couldn't sleep there. Some of the so-called Christians would crucify Christ all over again if he were ever foolish enough to go amongst them. At first our task looked easy enough. The bank of turf was only six foot wide and ten foot long. We were all set to go when he came out again. He was a medium-sized man who had a faintly superior air of the farmer-cum-shopkeeper class. A pillar of the Church, he would live and die a hypocrite. He despised drink but didn't mind selling it and using the proceeds to send his son off to Dublin University. He was going bald around the front and you could already see the middle-aged man peeping out behind the young man's frame.

'Ah, good, lads,' he called, 'now before you start digging I thought it as well to tell you how far down I want you to go. Well, naturally I want as much as it's safe to get out without having the banks collapse in on top of you. Now I was thinking that about sixteen spits would be plenty.'

'Hey, look here,' said Power, 'that's about ten feet down.'

'Ah, you're right there; ten foot or thereabouts. Still that's what I want, and I wouldn't have you working under a cloud.'

We looked at each other but there was no choice. We had nothing left, not a penny, and if ever we wanted to get to hell out of here, we needed that six quid. I decided to try another stroke.

'Look here,' I said, 'can't you let's have a bit of grub then before we start? I haven't eaten anything in four days.'

He pondered on this, his greedy little mind wondering how he could twist us. 'Right,' he called, 'I will have my father come out first thing in the morning with some grub.'

In the morning! But that left us nothing for tonight. Then we sent Corky down to a labourer's cottage to ask for a drink of water. It worked, the woman asked him if he wouldn't like some milk. Eventually he came back with a huge, hot griddle cake and a large jug of milk. May that good woman live to a thousand, and may her and all about her keep well till the tenth generation.

That night, I nearly burned to death. Finding nowhere to sleep we built a fire round the edge of the bank and lay down round it. In the middle of the night I must have turned over because I was awakened by Corky pulling me through a stream. The whole bottom half of my raincoat was burned away. The heat must have lulled me to sleep because I never knew a thing.

The next day the man's old father came out and the food that he brought with him was a small pan loaf and about four ounces of corned beef. Old Ryan was making sure that he didn't pauperise himself. We scoffed it all in about five minutes and then looked back wearily at the hole. We had run into a snag.

About five feet down, there was a piece of bog oak. It was in fact the roots of a primeval tree that had never really rotted with all the other vegetation in that long ago age when dinosaurs had nibbled at their tops. With the old man sitting like a little fairy making sure that we cut every sod, we had to scrape our way round it the best we could. This meant that I had to try and cut turf and throw it up the bank with the long arm of the tree sticking into my back.

The next day we got down about nine feet and the water started to pour in behind us. The bog, which holds millions of gallons of water wrapped up in its belly, starts to empty it into the first hole it can find. To save losing turf usually the cutter builds himself a little dam which holds back the water behind him. This is a tricky business. Men have been buried alive under a sudden rush of water and several tons of wet bog. The old man was anxious that we got the last scrap. I was cutting the last sods when I thought that I saw the soft, brown wall at my back bulge as though someone were running his hand down and along it. Then the whole wall just crumbled away and a flood three or four feet high came pouring in. In my excitement, I raced against the walls of my tomb, but my hands just scraped the soft slush down. Then Corky shoved the handle of a slean down and shouted 'Here, Ginger, grab this.' As I did, I felt the sludge snake in around my feet. Almost running up the handle of the pole, I felt my shoe pull off and looking down I saw it vanish under tons of bog. As I sat on the bank I didn't know whether to laugh or cry. Finally I took off my other shoe and flung it in after the first. 'Good man, yourself,' said Corky, 'and may your bad luck go with it.'

That night we picked up our six quid and headed back to Dublin. On the train going home, my stockinged feet were no problem. It was as I got out that they became a nuisance. Because it was a wet day they became long and floppy. Then they tended to pull forward and slap up and down like a clown's boots. But then I had the choice of that or going barefoot. The bare feet were out; I had tried that, and hundreds of kids had gathered round me to ask what monastery I was going to do penance in. So with my stockings beating the ground in front of me, I made my way home.

CHAPTER TEN

The Turf Game

IT WAS just before Christmas when our Sean told me his plan. We were to set up in business. With our economic rears secured we could really afford to wage war on capitalism. We had a choice of a number of ventures. A fag shop? Buying and selling pigs? Or the turf game? 'On the turf,' in Ireland, can mean either a bookie or a bogman. We settled for turf because so many had started with an ass and cart and now were the masters of vast fleets of motor lorries. All we had to do was to buy it at thirty bob a ton and flog it for three and a half quid. Our only problem was one of transport. Petrol and our money being rationed, horses seemed the logical answer. A mate of ours, Murphy, had money—lots of it, being a psychoanalyst.

He advanced us £100 on the strict understanding that every penny profit would be divided equally in our co-op. 'Of course, of course,' we murmured, feeling like men about to make millions. Alas, like every venture I have ever tried, elements of farce intruded very quickly. Our horses must have thought they had fallen into the hands of madmen. The first one we bought was a great big, ugly mare named Polly. She seemed to be a cross between a giraffe and an elephant. Clever men that we were, we bought the cart before the horse. The result was we couldn't fit Polly into her cart, however we tried. She just couldn't get in between the shafts. Eventually we decided to leave the shafts high in the air pointing towards heaven. Even so, Polly was too long in the body, with the result that every time the undercarriage came forward it tapped Polly smartly across the heels, making her jump forward like a ticklish girl.

Well, we determined to parade out and try our luck. Unfortunately we had to go down Winetavern Street Hill, which all Dublin knows is very steep. Every few yards of our journey the cart would hit Polly and she'd jump like a circus pony. The hill at that time was infested with lazy idlers, cattle-dealers and gypsies. As we made our way down they laughed and jeered at us. Their advice ranged from 'take it to the knackers' and 'get down and milk it,' to 'let's make the next dance a waltz.' Mortified, we had to return as rapidly as possible to base. Being men of vision (politically, that is) we saw no reason to stop our expansion because of this little mishap. We determined to let Polly lie abed for a while and buy a pony to fit our cart. Determined not to be caught again we enlisted the aid of an ex-I.R.A. man-cum-horse-dealer, Pat Flynn by name. This Flynn was the sort of man you took to be a pillar of sense. In fact he was a very simple, easily gulled fellow.

Pat, large and commanding in the pub the night before, looked strangely ill at ease when confronted by the animal itself. After a few trial runs I pointed out that the pony seemed to have wa-wa legs. When he ran he threw his front legs out sideways instead of to the front. This made him look for all the world like the leader in the Black and White Minstrel Show, singing 'Mammy.' The horse-dealer, Dunphy, was an evil-looking man. His eyes, darting here and there, were fascinating. In his hands he held a stick about three foot long that looked more for business than pleasure. Beside him stood two go-betweens, so called. Really they were part of his gang who pretended to be passing by and were now demanding fair play for all. Occasionally Dunphy would pretend to walk away, only to be drawn back by one of these wretches imploring him to return and not 'do the young fellows the unkindness.' The other one was more subtle. He alternated between telling us how ridiculously low our price was and abusing Dunphy for sticking to his.

Dunphy had a wide-brimmed hat and under it an immense yellow scarf. With his trousers hooked up over his boots he looked like a Tibetan. In a loud voice he dismissed my charge of wa-wa legs. Glaring at me, he said: 'Ah, but mister Flynn here will know what I'm talking about.' Our Pat just nodded dumbly.

Like Stalin, the gypsy had a way of turning hard or soft as the situation demanded; now he suddenly smiled at me and asked would I do him the favour of taking a glass of porter. Flattered that I was now the centre of attraction, away I went with him. In the pub I was amazed at how generous he was. We couldn't get near our pockets to buy a round. A half-dozen drinks later he threw down a bundle of notes and asked us did we think he was worried about a paltry twenty. This did the trick with me; I've never been able to believe that a rich man would rob me. Ten drinks later he had our twenty quid and we had the lady-stepper. The next day we yoked him and called him Marshal Tito. At first everything was sound. He fitted the cart a treat. Happy at last, we loaded up and set out to do a sale. Alas, just going over Dolphins Barn Bridge he collapsed. Now I have always loved animals, especially horses, but with everything that had happened I felt desperate and began to drag Tito to his feet. A woman passing by started to screech and bawl, threatening us with the police.

'You dirty beast,' she roared, 'leave the poor animal be.' I tried to reason with her, pointing out that we had deliveries to make.

'Then,' she sneered, 'why don't you pull the cart yourself? You look big and ignorant enough to do it.'

To my amazement my brother Sean took her seriously.

'All right,' he said, 'I'll stay here with Tito while you pull the cart along—it's only another couple of hundred yards.' After violent debate I agreed. But just as I was heaving and straining our Sean came up beside me and standing outside the shafts reproved me, saying.,

'Don't just walk along like that, shout out "Turf for sale" as you go.' In a fury I flung down the cart smashing the two shafts. But, like gambling, business is a fever: no matter how much you lose you try to get it back. In our case Murphy kept us supplied with the cash reserves for further madness. Our cart we repaired and while our horses continued their two-hour week we canvassed for fresh customers. Being socialists, we stood for the ending of exploitation for everyone, including the horses.

They were as far as it was possible to be equal partners in our co-op. Of course they couldn't join us in the pub for our daily meetings, but at least we were determined that they should be well fed. Where we stabled our nags was also a food emporium. In all innocence we asked the merchant to advise us on the nature and amounts of horse food. After a moment's silence to commemorate the advent of looneys, he replied.

'Well, I would recommend half a stone of whole oats per meal three times a day with a stone of hay at night.'

'Is this for each horse?' I asked him.

'Yes,' he smiled, 'and that will keep them in prime condition.'

They were in prime condition all right, in fact by the end of the week they were leaping out of their skins. With no work and tons of grub they became very playful. Indeed Polly grabbed me twice by the arm and nearly kicked me to death. At the end of the second week we found that our feed bill was running at the rate of two pounds per horse per week. All thoughts of work vanished from the nags' heads and they simply refused to let us yoke them for honest toil. To all our entreaties Polly simply turned a great big bottom and let fly with her enormous hooves.

Our stableman was something of a Hitler and wouldn't tolerate such nonsense for one minute. Like all small men he was afflicted with delusions of grandeur. One morning he advised us to stop this mollycoddling and get down to business. Pushing me out of the way he proceeded in his jodhpurs to confront Polly with a whip about twenty foot long. As he walked in to her stall he threw up the whip in a commanding fashion and ordered Polly to leave her warm bed. Unfortunately for him his whip got caught in the rafters and Polly seized him across the back with her great yellow teeth. Much to my delight I had to save him, letting Polly get a good bite first, though. With the aid of two corporation dustmen we eventually succeeded in getting the anarchist horse safe within the shafts and, with the two of us hanging on the reins, we made our way to Crumlin. Giving tongue to our cry, 'Turf for sale, Turf for sale,' we soon had a nice little queue of customers at the back of our cart.

Just beside us was a building site and, just as one poor woman was leaning forward to lift down her seven pounds of fuel, Polly reared up and backed away from the swinging jib of a crane. The cart came back scattering our patrons to all sides and forcing them to jump for dear life into a great muddy trench. Appalled, I shouted to Sean, 'For God's sake, let's get to hell out of here or they'll murder us when they get up.' In his enthusiasm Sean hit Polly too hard and I last saw him clinging to Polly as best he could as the cart flew out of sight down the road.

We were at tea when there came a knock on the door. The copper said, 'I'm sorry, Ma'am, but one of your boys has been taken to hospital after being thrown from a runaway horse and cart.'

Poor old Sean. He looked half dead when I saw him, face pale, his head bound up in a huge bandage. I thought he had had his lot. Groaning, he moaned, 'Do you know that crazy horse could find nothing better to run into than a telegraph pole?'

Sean, slight and bespectacled, was cut out by nature for more scholarly pursuits. He would have looked more at home lecturing in Trinity College than hauling turf, but he was dogged as a terrier. I had hoped that the accident would prove a blessing and that now at last the agony would end. Not a bit of it: Sean seemed to be driven even madder by the knock on the head. This can happen; I knew a man once who joined the Communist Party after a whack of a brick.

It seemed now that our business had been on too small a scale to prosper.

'Let's hire a barge,' says Sean, 'and float several hundred tons of turf direct from the bog, thereby eliminating the middleman and making a fortune.' And so an old canal barge was hired and with Flynn as captain we loaded her up and set sail for Guinness's harbour. On the way I noticed that either the water was getting deeper or we were shrinking; in any case we were a lot lower in the water after every lock. Just outside the harbour is a narrow entrance which barely holds a boat—indeed with a bigger one you barely scrape through. I thought to warn 'captain,' who now sported a sou'wester and a hooky pipe.

Rolling with the barge he laughed me to scorn, shouting, 'We'll go through there like a dose of salts.' Seizing the tiller, we made straight for the gap—but with bad luck, a sudden gust of wind threw us to one side and we hit the entrance wall with a thunderous crack. A violent lurch and we stopped and commenced to sink rapidly. Flynn, in the best tradition of the sea, jumped for the bank. Joining him there, we stood and gazed at the barge and cargo effectively blocking the whole channel.

'By God,' said Flynn gravely, 'there'll be a porter famine in the Midlands tomorrow.'

Shortly after, the final meeting of our co-op was held. Murphy had almost gone mad from worry and was using most unseasonable language. Frothing away, he brandished a claim from the port and docks board for the sum of £300 being due for harbour clearance. Crestfallen, we told him we were finished, but what about the horses? We owed a month's feed bill and the yard man was striking them off rations. In a few choice words Murphy told us what we would do with Polly and Tito. Our Sean didn't like this one bit: 'I am ashamed,' he said, 'to see brother Willis Murphy weaken in the struggle.'

Still Murphy had left us and what could we do? In any case bad luck dogged his steps for all his cruelty. (The following year he was caught by his mother and father dancing in the nude in a Paris nightclub.)

'I'll tell you what,' says Sean. 'Public shame is what's wanted to bring that fellow back to his responsibilities, and that's what he's going to get.'

The following morning was Christmas Day. Our hearts grew heavy thinking of our poor brother nags' hungry day.

'Right,' says Sean, 'take them out and away we go for a little walk.' I noticed that we were heading for Rathmines, a prosperous part of Dublin. In a lovely Georgian square Sean halted and peered at the numbers on the gates.

'This is the one,' he shouted, 'through here.'

He motioned to me and up the gravel we went, leading a horse apiece. Like all the rich, the people in this house were eating in their front room. Loosing our pals, we watched them wander across the well-kept lawn and stand, faces pressed tight to the french windows. Raising his glass for a toast, brother Murphy's eye met the reproachful gaze of Polly. Struck quite dumb, his glass clattered to the ground. Polly, thinking that hostilities had commenced, turned a contemptuous rump, and with two blows of her hooves shattered the windows in around the guests. The centrepiece of the Murphy dinner was a large turkey bedecked with greenery. Tito daintily picked his way through the broken glass and, seizing the turkey, made off down the garden. I didn't wait to see what happened next, but picked up my heels and made off.

CHAPTER ELEVEN

Pastoral Picket

BY NOW I was getting deeper and deeper into a Marxist grouping based on released, left-wing I.R.A. men. One of them had begun to organise the dairy boys. God knows they needed organisation. Treated worse than the cattle they milked, they were a savage crew. At the time it was nothing for them to have to work seventy hours a week for as little as four pounds.

At first our efforts to organise them were a great success. In hundreds they poured into the union hall to hear that farmer after farmer had signed up with their union.

All except one. On him we turned our fire, determined to smash this last bit of resistance. I and a fellow called McGoon were assigned to picket his gate. As I walked up and down outside Farmer Brophy's gate, I wondered how in hell I had got caught up in such lunacy. Brophy had evidently pondered the question even more. I hadn't gone ten paces when he burst out upon me like an angry bull. Brandishing his crutch aloft he demanded to know why I was posing as a striking farm-hand.

'By the cut of you,' he sneered, 'you've never been nearer a cow than a bottle of milk.'

Stung by the truth of this sally, I roared back, 'It doesn't matter where I come from. You're in dispute with the farmworkers union whether you like it or not and I'm here as a member of the Dublin Revolutionary League to show solidarity.'

However, when he turned on my mate I did feel somewhat embarrassed. My mate was a civil servant. By day he collected taxes to buttress a State that by night he tried to knock down. At the sight of him Farmer Brophy almost collapsed with laughing. It was true he looked even less of a farmer's boy than me. For one thing he sported a long red beard. For another, in defiance of convention, he had allowed his hair to grow shoulder length.

'By God,' laughed Brophy, 'heaven help the poor cow that sees you, she'll lose a year's growth.'

McGoon just ignored him. Smiling into his beard, he clutched his picket-poster with renewed fervour. Brophy now began to walk round and round McGoon. Leering and sneering, he called upon the masses to witness their self-appointed saviour. His rude and vulgar serfs all dutifully echoed their master's voice. One of them loudly inquired where McGoon had got his fancy dress. It was true McGoon had overdone his disguise as a worker. I had warned him that morning that the toilers had long since given up the wearing of navvy hard-core trews tied at the knees. He had topped this outfit with a filthy cap of truly barbarous design. Emboldened by their master's teasing, the toilers began to pelt poor McGoon with large pieces of cow dung. He turned and, with saintly resignation and using his poster as a shield against the hail of dung, he murmured.

'They're backward, Brian; really backward; semi-fascist I shouldn't wonder.'

Inside the gate a spate of feverish activity commenced. A couple of minutes later out came Brophy triumphantly astride his milk-cart like a Roman charioteer. As he flew by he called to us to keep an eye on the place while he was out delivering the milk. Crestfallen, we returned to base to report to our leader that the picketing seemed to be a dead loss. Fanagen was a man who never admitted defeat till all his youthful disciples lay dead in the dust. Small of stature and funny to look at, he held our allegiance by his ability to talk longer and louder than anybody else. Also, he was constantly discovering plots, plots within plots, and counterplots, and traitors and police spies and enemies threatening the movement from within until nobody in our small band trusted anybody but Fanagen. He could, by invoking the sacred names of Marx and Engels, invest the most fantastic of schemes with logic and reason. As for the old political jargon, he could weave it like a regular magician and with a 'militant defeatism' here and a 'dynamic of history' there he could make pathetic defeat into resounding victory and a mass meeting of one tramp and a copper at the back of an empty hall seem like a significant step forward for the forward-moving, backward-looking popular, peace-loving masses.

He became a revolutionary in a fit of spite brought on by his failure to make a pile selling holy pictures door to door. Now he strode up and down, scowling at the floor. Suddenly he swung on us.

'Comrades,' he barked, 'Brophy's resistance must be smashed. The dairy boys are, by the very nature of their employment, a backward-looking section. It is up to us, of the politically-enlightened proletariat, to lead the way.'

So the next day saw us back again at Brophy's gate as he cantered by for the morning delivery. According to plan, we tumbled into Fanagen's French-gangster Citroen and, shoving our posters through the windows, gave chase. The plan was to picket each house that Brophy was to deliver at, but unfortunately our engine stalled just as we were nearing the houses. Frantically pushing McGoon out with the starting handle, Fanagen shouted, 'Come on man, he'll get away.'

Whether it was the engine or his beard or both, I couldn't say, but McGoon seemed to have a terrible job with the handle. Every time he bent over a great hank of hair fell down, making him grope for it like a blind man. Seeing our predicament, Brophy laughed his head off.

'There you are,' he shouted, 'they want to organise the bloody earth and they can't even get an oul' car going.'

Fanagen's next move was to hire bikes. Putting them against Brophy's mare, we were soon bowling along behind him. Our procession was an amazing sight. First came Brophy, then us; posters held on high. Next a village policeman who cursed the day and hour we were born. After that poured a horde of kids on bone-shakers, making a fearful din. As each door opened, the housewife looked up to see a mad-eyed McGoon brandishing his poster above Brophy's head. After about twenty deliveries, Brophy was nearly going mad trying to explain McGoon was not, and never had been, in his employ, and that he paid his men as well as he could do without charging more for the milk.

His face twisting with hatred, he foamed, 'Well, you can come to my next house and good luck to you.'

His next house was the new police station. It was a massive place, watched over by a police sergeant: six feet tall and three feet wide. I started to take down my poster, but McGoon wheeled on me.

'What do you think you're doing?'

'We can't carry on picketing here,' I said.

'Here' was a main road and a junction of three more.

'Indeed we can,' he replied, 'if the police are content to drink black milk they must take the consequences.'

And the consequences was that half of Dublin stopped to gaze at the novel sight of a picket outside a police station. Traffic was jammed for miles around.

Bus drivers couldn't believe their eyes. 'Police on strike?' and 'Picketing?' 'Will you look at that?' said one. 'Jaysus, they don't look much without the uniform.' The crowd was most eager to know how long we would be out. One rascal, Dinny Byrne, a thief of many years' standing, implored us not to weaken, but to stick it out, like men. Some instinct made me look behind, and there bearing down on us was a face like wrath itself—the sergeant. Thrusting my poster into someone's hands, I was away through the crowd. My last impression was that of McGoon being hauled by his beard to the station (which is why all serious revolutionaries should be clean-shaven).

In a frenzy, Fanagen decided on a public meeting to denounce Dicky Brophy. Quite a few people turned up and all went well at first. Fanagen painted a gripping picture of Dicky's men shivering in filthy lean-to's while they milked their beasts. Dramatically he warned of the threat of poisoning to all those who persisted in drinking the infected milk. A shout from the back interrupted his spiel. Brophy, crutch held aloft like a crusader, cleared a path right up to the platform. Loudly he called upon God to witness that he had never poisoned man nor boy in thirty years. The more he roared, the more he prodded the platform, and suddenly it toppled taking poor Fanagen with it. Solemnly Brophy intoned, 'It was the hand of God that downed that lying rascal.'

Meanwhile I had spotted a new menace in the shape of a large group of religious fanatics. They were carrying huge posters depicting the cross being smashed by hammer and sickle, and the inscription 'Choose—which is it to be?' Quick as a flash I clapped my mouth to the ear of a staunch Catholic and asked him was he going to tolerate the impudence of these Communists.

'Why so?' he asked.

'Why there,' I said, pointing to the fanatics. 'There they are, the dirty animals, parading out with their posters showing our cross being done down with their hammer and sickle.'

After scratching his head, he roared, 'I declare to God you're right,

they won't be there for long; on my oath they won't!' And letting out
a howl, he seized one of the posters and began belabouring the unfortunate owner about the head. The more the man denied he was a
Communist, the more he was beaten as a liar. Inspired by my friend's
example, the crowd waded into what was left of his companions.

With Brophy gaining the day, the ranks of our supporters dwindled
and Fanagen was driven to despair, deciding that terrorism was the
only answer. Giving me an old Colt automatic and McGoon a small
French pistol, he outlined his plan. We were to hire a taxi to take us to
the farm and to evict the driver on the way. Then we were to capture
Dicky, strip him naked, and tar and feather him (a punishment usually
reserved for landlords and traitors) and dump him down in the middle
of O'Connell Street. To me, the most revolting part of this plan was
to have to look at Dicky's naked stump.

So we met, late that night, down by the river: the pavements were
wet and deserted and the distant booming of ships in docks lent a dream-
like quality to the whole affair. Eventually, an empty taxi came along.

'Where to,' asked the driver.

'Out to Green Hills, mate,' said McGoon, making to get into the
cab. But the cabby barred his way.

'That's thirty bob there and back. I'm afraid I'll have to see the
colour of your money,' and looking at McGoon, he went on, 'I've
been caught by some queer old jokers before now, you know.'

Hurriedly we turned our pockets out. Between us we had four-and-
sixpence.

The taxi disappeared down the quay. Slowly I became aware of the
drizzle running down my face and soaking my collar. A picture of our
kitchen, warm and cheerful, came into my mind, and I realised that I
was starving with hunger. Fanagen was standing under a lamp-post polishing his specs with great concentration. Trying not to catch his eye, I
dropped the gun into his pocket and, murmuring something about
catching my bus, I made off. Just as I reached the corner I heard his voice.

'A skirmish, McGoon,' he was saying, 'historically insignificant; now
I've been watching the situation in building very closely and I think we
should prepare for the big struggles of the future. I think a leaflet. . .'

I rounded the corner and ran, like hell, for the bus. Ran away from
milk strikes to . . . the army.

CHAPTER TWELVE

Soldier On

I REJOINED the army to escape a sentence for my part in the dairy boys' union. I was charged with criminal conspiracy arising out of the Brophy case and went up for trial to Green Street Court. The judge hearing that I had in the meantime volunteered to serve my country, looked kindly on my young head. I was put on probation and returned to my army training.

As soon as I joined the army I sensed that the real power lay in the cook-house. Cooks were powerful men and cook-sergeants, well, even the orderly officers trembled to upset them. Of course, the root of their power lies in the fact that the army is a hungry place. The food may be good enough but there's never enough of it.

At eighteen I could eat a horse and then look round for the jockey. By dint of much conniving I managed to dodge manoeuvres and wangle my way into the field kitchen. My superior was a Private Sweeney. Sweeney was tall and plump, he had fat dewy lips and quick calculating eyes and he was the most wickedly lazy man. Lazy! He's the only person I have ever seen sweep a floor with his hands in his pockets; the brush handle stuck up his belt.

On the first morning we spent a pleasant hour sitting one either side of a churn and toasting each other in milk. Then we slowly made our way back to the main cook-house to pick up a tea boiler. Here, the cook-sergeant, Blake, had some bad news for us.

'Sorry lads,' he cried, 'I've had to use the boiler for cooking the week-end bacon.'

Looking into it, it seemed as though he had cooked a whole herd of pigs in it. Starting from the top went ring after ring of thick grease. Dismayed, I looked at Sweeney. He just waved a podgy hand and said,

'Oh, that's all right, Sarge, we'll soon have that clean, it only needs a bit of elbow grease.'

'Rather you than me,' said Blake. 'Still, you're willing lads, here, take a few buckshee rations with you.'

He planked a couple of loaves and a half pound of butter down before us. As we ambled out to our base I grumbled, 'We'll never get that boiler cleaned in time for dinner, it's 11 o'clock now.' Sweeney munched away unconcernedly.

'Don't worry about it, it's very simple. When the water boils the grease will melt, right? Then we stick in the tea, colour it with loads of milk, and who's to know the difference.'

'Oh, I don't know,' I said apprehensively. 'They're bound to get that taste of the fat.'

'That lot? Taste the fat? Not likely; they're so hungry fool-acting about doing bear-crawls that they would eat the hind leg off a scabby dog.'

At first, all went well. The brown bog-water we used gave the mixture a fine dusky hue. But as it began to boil the grease came away in great chunks like icebergs in a thaw. Either there was too much grease or too little water. Whatever the cause, the stuff was now coagulating in a thick, heavy, sickening mass. Alarmed, I called Sweeney to have a look. Pursing his lips, he pronounced that the situation was grave, very grave indeed. Looking at the clock he said 'Well it's too late to brew a fresh lot now, this will have to do.'

Backing away, I protested: 'I'm not giving that stuff out, these Twenty-Second battalion mob will kill us.'

'Hm, I fear you're right.' He stared around him, absently pulling his lip.

As a shark has its pilot fish, so a cookhouse has its scavengers. Hungry men, they will do anything from bribery to dixie-scrubbing for a little extra grub. Such a one was Muzzy Moran. He was incredibly tall and thin and they called him Muzzy because he wasn't too bright up top. He always managed to be hanging around the cookhouse before and after meals; now he was standing outside our domain. Sweeney beckoned him over. 'Hey, Muzzy, here a minute.' As he shambled in, Sweeney handed him half a loaf and some butter. Unbelievingly, Muzzy hesitated. 'Go on,' cried Sweeney, 'take it.' As Muzzy wolfed it down, Sweeney stood right over him. 'Now, Muzzy, there's a little job you can help us with. Me and my mate here have to report to the

officers' mess. They need us to help with the serving.' I looked out of
the window as he went on. 'Now all we want you to do is serve the tea;
you'll be all right, there's nothing to it.' Moran shook his head vigorously in agreement. As we were going out of the door, Sweeney
said, with an evil grin on his face, 'Only one cup per man now, Muzzy,
and no favourites, no seconds till every man has had his first.'

Once outside I started to run. Pulling me by the shoulder, Sweeney
said, 'What's the hurry? Aren't you going to stop and see the sport?'

'Sport? You clown, they'll kill us when they see the tea.'

'Not us,' he laughed, 'Moran maybe, but not us; that tea's got
nothing to do with us.'

Turning off the road, he installed himself in a heather bank overlooking the hut. We hadn't long to wait. At twelve precisely the
hordes came tumbling down off the Common; laughing and whistling,
they shuffled quickly into an eager, sweating line, mugs swinging from
their web belts.

The first man grabbed his bread and shoved his mug under the tea
urn tap. Muzzy raised a warning hand importantly. 'Take your time
now; you'll all get served.' With a flourish he gave the tap a twist and
out came—nothing. Nonplussed, he shook the urn but still—nothing.

A waiting man said helpfully, 'Got some tea-leaves stuck in tap, eh?'

Frowning harassedly, like a busy housewife, Moran lifted the lid
and gave the tea a stir with the dolly-stick. Out it came, not in a stream
exactly, more like chunks, great, fat, independent lumps that went
plop, plop into the man's cup. At first, neither Moran nor the man
could move. Then lifting the lid, the man looked down into the pestifer-
ous depths. His cry of anguish brought half the company to see, and
smell, the horrible mixture. Almost automatically they began belabouring Muzzy who could only shield his head and hope for the best.

Beside me Sweeney was in convulsions. 'For God's sake,' I appealed
to him, 'keep quiet or they'll hear you and it'll be all up with us.' Too
late; one of the enemy had spotted Sweeney's big head. Hallooing to
each other, they started after us like hounds after a fox. I think we
knocked a few seconds off the half-mile record but even so we barely
managed to make the camp in front of them. Diving under the duck-
boards of the marquee that served as the main canteen, we lay and
listened to the searchers going to and fro enquiring the where-

abouts of the two cooks—only that wasn't quite what they called us.

'Now what are we going to do?' I said.

'Well,' he pondered, 'the main thing for us now is to reach the digger alive and give ourselves up to the M.P.s. Otherwise, I'm afraid that those ungrateful swine will make mincemeat out of us.'

Wriggling forward, I took a peep to see how the land lay. It lay very well indeed. Right before my eyes were two of the loveliest legs I had ever had the good fortune to clap my eyes on.

'Aha,' smiled Sweeney, 'the girls have come to entertain the soldier-laddies. Well, well, well, that gives me an idea.'

'Yes,' I scowled, 'and I know all about your ideas.'

'No listen, don't be like that, as soon as these women move off, we can creep in and tog ourselves in their gear.'

'What do you take me for?' I asked.

He lay back. 'All right then, take your chances with that lot out there, but, remember, they don't think it's very funny to get tea like ours with nothing else till six o'clock tonight.'

Ten minutes later I was attired as an old Irish washer woman, complete with shawl tied tightly round my head. To give Sweeney his due, his get-up was far more artistic than mine. He tightened in his waist, blackened his eyelashes and lipsticked his already feminine lips till he looked quite the part. With a thin squeak he called 'Come on, dear, let's take the air.'

We might have got clean away with it but that clown had to start winking roguishly at some old sweats polishing their gear outside the tent.

'Hey, love,' called one, 'taking anyone with you?'

'I might,' simpered Sweeney.

Quick as a flash the soldier had his arm round Sweeney who immediately tried to repel the soldier's clutching hands.

'Now, now,' he squealed, 'leave a decent girl alone.'

A corporal who had been watching disapprovingly suddenly became suspicious and began to move over to us, and Sweeney minced away rapidly towards the women's toilets. I tried to follow but found I couldn't move; my dress was caught in a tent peg and I didn't dare look round. I knew if the corporal got a close look of my face I was a goner.

He was right behind me when he shouted 'Halt! About turn!' And I did, instinctively. Before I could save myself a horny hand shot out and pulled my skirt down. 'You filthy bastard,' he shouted, 'By God, you'll see how we treat bloody pansies in this man's army.'

Lucky for me, I played football for my C.O., or I would have been charged with importuning. As it was, the charge that was finally read out was: 'Private J. Sweeney and Private B. Behan did on June 10th, 1944, attempt to render their comrades unfit for military duties in that whilst acting as cook orderlies they served tea that was unfit for human consumption.' Penalty: fourteen days' detention.

This was my first whack of the army nick. The cells were huge and the wooden beds folded in the middle and would engulf you if you slept unwarily. Still I determined to sleep my brains out and forget all about cooks and cookhouses. I was just getting off to a nice nap when I felt myself being prodded like a sheep in a pen. Angrily I lifted my head to look into the face of an extremely irate guard commander.

'What the hell do you think you're on, man?'

Trying to lie at attention and salute at the same time, I answered, 'Well, sir, I just thought I would try and get some sleep.'

Behind him, the sergeant of the guard beat a tattoo on the legs of the bed with his cane. 'Feet on the floor, man, feet on the floor. You're not lying in state receiving visitors.'

Angry now, I reluctantly stood up.

'Don't you know,' barked the officer, 'that no one round here goes to bed till I say so. Is that clear?'

Surlily I muttered, 'What's the good of me hanging round here all night with nothing to do?'

'Nothing to do, eh—sergeant, can we arrange for our friend's mind to be kept occupied?'

Grinning evilly, the sergeant reappeared with two buckets of cold water and planked them down beside me. Then he came with a scrubbing brush which he slung beside the buckets. 'There now, Behan, start scrubbing. I want this cell scrubbed from top to bottom before morning.'

Groaning, I started to scrub the stone flags; all my spite and hatred were directed towards Sweeney. Knowing him, I had a strong suspicion that he had somehow wriggled out of the sentence, and in my frenzy I imagined him lying safe and sound in some warm bed while I looked down into a bucket of dirty, freezing water. Glaring at the floor, I began to think of all the tortures that I might inflict upon him. I prayed that he might die roaring. 'Oh God,' I thought, 'may the hair round his testicles turn into hammers and beat his brains out.' This thought so pleased me that I soon had my task finished and fell into bed at 2 o'clock in quite a happy frame of mind

The Irish army never fired a shot in anger in its life. During the war we stood ready to drive back the combined might of the Germans and the British. With no fighting, football and other field sports were our main preoccupation. I played for two teams—the army during the week, and a civilian team on Sundays. That is, on the Sundays I wasn't speaking at public meetings in O'Connell Street.

On Sundays I tied my boots on the handle-bars of my bike and cycled off. On this particular day it was a fine, warm sunny morning. I had to thread my way carefully through the crowds that streaked the roads leading to Mass. Soon I was leaving the city and heading out on the coast road. On my left was the tiny graveyard of Killbarrack. Here lay an old friend of my mother's forever looking out to Dublin Bay. I stopped a while, but couldn't find her grave. She had died as she had lived—timid, unknown and unnoticed.

Our football grounds were just off the Malahide Road, within shouting distance of the sea. Green and flat, the pitch tempted you to take off your clothes and roll like a horse. At every corner the slight breeze stretched the little marking flags full out. Our team was based on a tiny huddle of labourers' cottages that stood in the shadow of Howth Head. Of course, our whole team didn't come from there. Five of us were army men, with a sprinkling of garage hands and farm labourers. In two years we had gone from bottom of the league to the semi-finals of the county championship. Team after team we had destroyed, routed and crushed, till now the cup stood within touching distance.

In the dressing room I was pushed and jostled as I tried to get a jersey that wasn't torn or marked. By now I was on good terms with all the team. Because we were partners only in sport we saw the very best sides of each other. It was a pleasure just to get ready with them. Underneath the fun and games you felt the common pull of a common effort. You valued all the men there in a different way. Little Tommy O'Connor I remembered because of his curious bobbing and weaving that had buried goal after goal in our enemies' hearts.

'My heavens, but it was a rasper,' he would laugh.

As game as a badger, he went in no matter what. How many times had I lifted him off the ground after some full-back had piled into him. Larry Anderson I prided in because he was our last line. After him came our goal; but it was a very able forward who went past Larry. Billy Lynch was our Kid Galahad. Tall, blond, good looking, he drank like a fish. Erratic in football and women he was a constant source of worry to us. Jack was a brown nut of a man who worked as a hod carrier all week. To knock up against him was to know you had hit off something solid. Our wealthiest man was Billy Maguire. His aunt opened a garage and to us he seemed of the very rich. But he was in no way stand-offish, and was a smooth, polished performer.

I had been football-mad for years. At the slightest sign of a match I would go miles just to look at it. Like the boy in the story, when I was good I was very good, but when I was bad I stank. Two years of constant battle had hardened and sharpened us to knife edge. We knew just where we were likely to find who with low or high balls. We knew not to panic when the flock were scattered and the wolves were diving in amongst us. We had that indefinable thread that binds a real team together. In this championship we had come within seconds of defeat. We had learned to rally after a bad body-blow early on. We were a team.

Gaelic football is played with fifteen men. It is really a cross between soccer and Rugby. As in Rugby, you can catch the ball, but it's much faster, having no scrums. Unlike the soccer, the ball can be kicked from the hands, giving the goal-keeper no particular advantage. As we massed for the throw-in I saw why our opponents had reached the semi-final. They looked as if they had all come out of the same machine. Unlike our crowd, where the ages went from eighteen to thirty-five, with two married and one on the verge, this lot were all about eighteen to twenty-two, and looked virgins. They seemed as flinty and as hard as rocks, and looked equally indestructible.

The man who came back to mark me was ginger-haired like myself. I nodded fraternal greetings to him, which he acknowledged with a grunt. Then just as I was running forward with a ball he pretended to punch it out of my arms, and instead, gave me a couple of piledrivers right into the soft underbelly over my thighs. For a second I thought I would never get up after the pain. Slowly it subsided, and I saw the bastard standing over me with a grin, saying, 'Sorry, but I was going for the ball.'

So that was it. He was just telling me to lie down and let him get on with it. I smiled back. 'Oh, I am all right now.'

Contemptuously, he lifted me groggily to my feet. I kept away from him for a while. Then he ran forward to catch a high, lobbing ball. Away he sailed in a lovely leap, hoping to have it all to himself. I bunched my fist and ran after him. Just as he was going to catch the ball I pretended to try and punch it from between his hands. Instead I belted him squarely across the butt of the head, knocking him quite unconscious. When he came to he found me the most solicitous of opponents. I hovered round, repeating again and again, 'Sorry, friend, but I was aiming at the ball.' He got the message, and we began to play a nice clean game.

From the start it was obvious we were up against it. The other side were mainly based around a college and they didn't spend their weekends supping beer. They ran like greyhounds, until it seemed they must run us into the ground. At midfield they had two giants. One was about six foot three, and the other was a little shorter but broader. They weren't just fast, they had a movement, a combination that took the ball from their own goal right to ours.

Our supporters were getting frantic. Small though the hamlet was, they turned out, man, woman and child, no matter where we went. And we didn't just play the game and shove off. First they took us to the pub, and we drank and relived the match until porter spilled over and ran down our noses. Then they took us home and lushed us up with a dirty great dinner. In many ways, being army men, the team became our second home. As soon as it became dark off we went to a dance hall that looked out over Howth Harbour. Our girl supporters would walk us back through moon-swept cornfields to the little lonely station that carried us back to our billet.

At half-time our trainer, Jack Breen, called us together.

'It's no good, lads, they have the edge on us at centre field. If we don't break their combination up we might as well lie down and die.' Turning to me he said, 'Now, Ginger, I want you to go in midfield with Tom O'Brien. Don't try and catch anything; they're too big. Punch everything away, then do something; only don't let them walk all over you.'

My old heart glowed with pleasure. To be the one called on in the fatal hour was for me the dream that I had had time and again, of leading great noble armies to battle. At first our enemies caught all round them. I decided to get behind and punch the ball out of their hands. But it was no good. Every time I went up for a ball the lofty fella had the slight edge that made all the difference. Again and again they beat us, sending low, long, raking balls lobbing into our goal mouth. But for Larry Anderson and Maguire we were finished.

As it was only a question of time before they cracked under this terrific pressure, somehow or other we had to break the even swing of the ball right into our square. We had to break their strangle-hold at midfield. Another kickout came from our hard-pressed defenders. Again they seemed to pluck the ball right down out of the sky. Then I resolved to try and catch with them. There seemed no other way of doing anything. On the face of it, it seemed impossible. That extra four inches left my marker plenty of room to just lightly hop up and tear the ball down. Still, I determined to try it. Anything was better than looking at them helplessly while they beat our defence to a pulp.

I had found in training that if you ran a little before jumping it will give you a lift of at least a couple of inches. Again we lined up for the kickout. I ran back behind Lofty and waited for the ball. As the ball came out, strong and high, he went up, his two great paws out like a bear. Behind, I came running, hoping that I wouldn't misjudge the ball and land flat on my face. I sprang up until I felt I was sitting up on his shoulders. I felt my hands seize the ball and down I came. First I side-stepped his mate; then I swung round, dodging the half back. From the sidelines my little hamlet were screaming, 'For God's sake get rid of it.' 'Oh hell, lose it.' 'He's holding on to it too long.' 'Boot it! Boot it!'

Steadying up, I saw two full backs charging at me like bulls in a field. I sank my boot under the ball, lifting it long and high. The goalie, his face half blinded from the sun, shouted, 'Let it go, it's all right.' But it wasn't. Dropping suddenly and sharply it plummetted straight under the bar.

At the same time the two full backs hit me, and I felt as though I was jammed between two walls. Down I went on the hard, ridged turf till I thought my shoulder was smashed. But I managed to get up, and there at the other end I could see the linesman slowly raising the green flag for a goal. Little Tommy O'Connor ran up and was jumping all over me like a lunatic. From the sidelines I heard one of our old supporters shouting, 'Ah, good man yourself, Ginger. By the holy God tonight your blood's worth bottling.'

From then on we slowly bent our enemies' backs until we broke them into little pieces. We were in the final. That night the *Dublin Evening Mail* wrote, 'Ginger Behan was a tower of strength in midfield.'

In the final we collapsed. Stage fright they call it. Whatever the cause, in front of those huge stands, with all my family and friends watching, I couldn't do a thing right.

Deeply disappointed, it only made me all the more anxious to leave Ireland. Discharged from the army, it meant that now when I went out with the Stars I wasn't able to pay my way at the bar. I could see nothing in Ireland for me. All I had had for twenty years was heartbreak and hard work. England, with its tales of big money and small shovels, drew me on. At the same time I had lost my girl friend. With no money I found it impossible to keep going out. Ruthlessly, I drove her away from me. Time and again she turned up for dates to find me morose and miserable. Poor girl. She stood it for a couple of weeks and then she just didn't come any more. Perhaps it's my pride. All my life I had insisted that I would stand or fall alone, unaided. Eileen, tall and graceful, would have done anything just to have a quiet Dublin life, a small house, steady income, and away we would go. Again I found religion jumping up and down between us.

Denied equality, treated like unpaid landladies, Irish women turn more and more to religion as a consolation. Something warned me that I would never find happiness in such a set-up. I wrote her one or two mad, mad letters in which I traced our problems back to primitive Communism. Letters which she wisely ignored.

CHAPTER THIRTEEN

About Religion

AT FIRST I thought Baldy was joking. 'Me be your best man; you're pulling my leg?'

'No, I am not, Brian. It's a case of having to, and I feel too ashamed to ask any of the tribe to help me out.' This tribe consisted of our fellow army clerks. I became one in an effort to escape a maddened Platoon Commander.

He had taken our lot out on the square and attempted to teach us battle tactics. After lining us all up, he put a tin helmet in the middle and said, 'Now, lads, I want you to imagine that this is an enemy pill-box. Corporal Quinn, let's hear the command.' Quinn was a tall string of misery with one terrible handicap: he had the squeakiest voice you ever heard outside a woman.

First we had to call out 'No. 1 rifleman.' 'No. 2 rifleman.' Then 'No. 1 light automatic.' Then 'No. 2 light automatic.' I had to call out 'No. 1 bombardier.' Watching all this was our Commanding Officer, a Lieut.-Col. Paul.

As soon as the shout of our call had died away, Quinn marched out three paces and, pointing dramatically at the helmet, shouted 'Platoon will attack and kill all enemy there!' Unfortunately, from him it emerged as the silliest wail you've ever heard. It wouldn't frighten a grasshopper.

Of course, as usual, I couldn't keep my mouth shut. As soon as 'she' was finished, I called out 'Oh my God, but you're a fierce devil of a man.'

Anxious then to avoid strained relations, I volunteered for the Adjutant-General Staff, and surprisingly got in too.

Turning to Baldy, I said, 'Now look here, I don't mind doing best man for you, but you know what I think about religion. Why don't you try somone else?'

Baldy was so called because he came to us with his head shaved after doing a term in detention. What for, I never did find out. A farmer's boy, he had worked hard all his life to little or no avail. In the army, he found a lazy life, three good meals a day and quite reasonable pay. Reasonable pay that is for the single man.

The army frowns on married men. Its rates of pay are designed to keep the married man in constant poverty. Maybe they know that a married man will be less inclined to leave a nice warm bed and soft wife. A single man will do anything or go anywhere. After all, there's not much taste in nothing.

Taking another pull out of his cigarette, he said, 'Look, I have no choice; she's being put out of her digs. If we don't get married, she'll end up on the streets.'

'Look here,' I cried, 'what can I do? I haven't been in our parish church for ten years. Our parish priest is not exactly friendly with us you know.'

This was true. He had called one day and told my mother that we would go to hell. He had come at the right time. There were four of us sitting in the kitchen, all unemployed and hungry for spiteful argument. 'Come in, father, and tell them yourself,' said my mother. In he came: his fat, rounded face standing up from a heavy, fleshy neck that hung out in laps over his collar.

'God save all here,' he called.

'Ah, including the cat, father,' said Johnny Byrne, 'no discrimination, father.'

Looking round, he sat down heavily. 'Now,' he began, 'I have noticed that none of you lads attend your duties. For example, I never see one of you in church on a Sunday.'

At this, Johnny Byrne remarked 'I attend all my duties all right, father, but I don't think they include going to church. In my view, you're indistinguishable from the Communists. In fact, if I was to say anything it would be to say that you are a kind of medieval Communist Party.'

At this the priest burst out laughing. 'You're not serious, Mr Byrne, why we are daggers drawn with the Reds.'

'Oh you may be, but that signifies nothing, only that you are struggling for power. One of you is the dictator of the soul and the other is of the body. When the two of you get together then may God help us all.'

The priest was determined to give as good as he got. 'It seems strange, Mr Byrne, that you should be calling on a god to help you that you think is non-existent. But surely, even with your scientific mind, you will agree that there must have been a beginning to everything, and, accepting that, you will surely accept that God must have begun things.'

'Oh me God I don't,' retorted Byrne, 'you say there must have been a beginning. Well then which came first, the chicken or the egg?'

'This is ridiculous nonsense!' shouted the worthy father, belting off out of the door.

However, to get back to the matter in hand. 'Look,' pleaded Baldy, 'come with me tonight and meet Mary. Then make up your mind.'

I reluctantly agreed, and lay back to sleep. Around me the forms tossed and turned while, through the long windows, the moon came pouring in. Its light picked up the webbing hanging in strands over our heads. Down below I could hear the crunch of the flying patrol as they made their way round the blocks. It was a fact: compulsory religion like compulsory anything was something I wouldn't have. The army got round it by saying only the Church Parade was compulsory and the rest was optional. So I went on parade and stopped when we got to the door. I suffered for the rest of the week. By some odd chance, I found myself doing more and more guard duties. So I gave up and went inside.

Luckily word of this had not reached my local parish, or I would have never gone bail for Baldy. His bride-to-be was a very pretty, little girl.

'Now,' said Baldy, 'here she is, Brian, the cause of all my misfortunes. You'd never think she was up the pole, would you?'

Mary blushed, but I hastened to relieve her mind on my attitude. 'Don't mind him, Mary, there's many a man that would take his place in the dock.'

'You'll do it then?' queried Baldy.

Heavy hearted, I said 'Yes, and I'll get my mother to make up a little wedding breakfast as well.'

On the morning of the wedding, I nearly slept it out. Luckily, Baldy came round, and away we went. Just before we entered the holy place, he stuck an envelope in my hand.

'What's this, then?'

'Well you know I told this old priest that I would make an offering.'

'Make an offering? You must be crazy, Baldy. Why you only have a couple of quid to live on.'

'Oh never mind; let's not have a song and dance about this. For God's sake, just give it to him!'

'Oh well,' I said, 'if that's what you want.'

In we went and the thing soon began. In point of fact, I think there is far more dignity in a church wedding than in a register office one: that is, if you are going to have any ceremony at all. This one was soon over, and we adjourned to sign the register. The bride and groom went first, leaving me to sign and pay the offering. The more I thought about it, the more I was determined not to pay it. As I leaned over to sign, I laughed to think of the shock the priest was going to get in a minute. He laughed: thinking he was going to get some dough, and, of course, not knowing what I was laughing at.

'Well,' he remarked, 'a lovely wedding, and a lovely couple.'

'They are, father, that they are. Well goodbye now.'

I turned to go when he called apprehensively 'Haven't you forgotten something?'

Smiling, I said 'I don't think so, father.'

'Well, what about the offering for Holy Mother Church?'

'I am afraid, father, Holy Mother will have to do without in this case. You see, these young people are in dire straits. In fact they only have a couple of quid to start married life.'

At this he became quite angry. 'If they have only a couple of pounds they shouldn't be getting married. What are they going to live on?'

I was delighted. 'Ah,' I smirked, 'this is a very materialist way of looking at things. I thought that you would advocate that they should get married and that God would provide.'

'Never mind that,' he snarled, 'if they can't afford to give anything to the Holy Mother, surely they won't begrudge something for the sacristan. The man has six children.' To illustrate his point, he gestured to the worthy man who stood in the corner folding up the priest's vestments.

Unabashed, I retorted, 'Well I am not responsible for any of his children.'

'Look here,' said the priest, 'I have a good mind to go out after that young couple and see what they have to say about all this.'

'If you do,' I said savagely, 'then I will mount your pulpit and tell the people you are extorting money from people too poor to pay it.'

He looked and then just wheeled round and said 'Go, get out of here.'

Outside, the couple were standing in the morning sunshine. I proudly presented Baldy with the envelope.

'What's this?' he said.

'Why, it's your money. You didn't think I would give it to him?'

His wife, Mary, leaned over and snatched it out of his hand. Looking at me fiercely she said, 'You shouldn't try to rob the Church. No good will come of it.' And away she went. I saw her handing the envelope to the priest. Then, shading his eyes, he looked to see where it came from. Spotting me, he seemed to give a triumphant smile.

It was the time of the missions: when worthy priests dressed like monks descended on the garrisons. They believed that, as a result of mighty preaching, they would get the most hardened reprobate to repent and confess his sins. As is well known, Catholic Confession takes place in a little box in which the priest sits and cocks his ear to your mouth. This man had annoyed me. In a fit of drink, I determined to undo him.

Going into the box I muttered 'Bless me, father, I have sinned. It is fifteen years since my last confession.'

I heard a startled 'What's that? Fifteen years!'

Even then, I hesitated. Peeping out through the curtain, I saw that creature Sweeney still there. Our bet still stood, so I pressed on. 'Father, I have committed a most grievous sin, and I don't know how to tell you it.'

He just sighed and, resting his head in his hands, said, 'Oh, come now, son, tell me. I have heard the most awful of sins.'

'I am sure you have, Father, but I doubt whether you have heard anything like this.'

All ears now, he leaned forward. 'Now, my son, make up your mind to tell everything. Hold nothing back, and shortly you will be absolved.'

I coughed miserably. 'I am afraid, Father, it would take the Holy Father himself to absolve me.'

He was getting rather angry. 'Let me be the judge of what you have done. Let me see now. Is it swearing?'

'No, Father.'

'Is it to do with drink?'

'No, Father.'

'Well then, is it the old thing, the women?'

'No, Father.'

'Not, I hope,' his voice grew deep with disgust, 'not other men?'

'No, Father.'

'Well, for heaven's sake, what is it then?'

'It's beastery, Father.'

'Beastery? Are you crazy, man, what on earth is that?'

'Well, Father, it has to do with love of animals. You see, I have fallen in love with an ass . . . a she-ass though, Father, I hasten to add.'

I ran, and just beat him to the door.

The Fox Hunters

ONCE WHILE I was in the army I walked out on the Clondalkin
Road and met a crowd of fox hunters. I could see them coming down
off the hill, half a mile away. All shapes and sexes, all manner of horse,
big, fat, fine, stringy. In some peculiar way the horses seemed to match
their owners. Heavy-haunched women rode fat-arsed horses. Skinny
men on nervous spindly ones. Their leader, the master of the hunt, was
astride a great grey mare who looked as if she could pull or plough with
the best. She had a wide, deep chest and came thundering on throwing
her hooves up to level with her master's feet.

I hadn't spotted the fox but suddenly he broke cover, slid across the
road and through a gate not a yard from where I stood. Now he was in
a neat field of cabbages. Poor fox, he ran as though his heart would
burst, his eyes looking wildly round for a way of escape. I heard one of
the horse-women neighing with nervous excitement; 'We've got him
now, he's trapped.' Foxy didn't run straight, in panic he swerved and
dodged among the cabbages losing ground all the time. The hounds,
great brown and white things, came crashing along, tongues lolling and
tails up. For them it was just a game, for the fox a game with life or
death at the end.

The odds were a little unequal to my mind; twenty mounted
adults plus fifteen hounds all to catch a creature not above eighteen
inches long whose fat bushy tail was bigger than the rest of him put
together. My heart went out to him and on an impulse I slammed the
gate tight shut and leant on it. It was a high gate with barbed wire top
and bottom. The first rider came up smiling pleasantly expecting me to
move even with the dogs milling and whining all around me; he got
very angry. At first he tried to frighten me with his horse, edging it
almost on top of me. This didn't worry me. I was well used to horses,
some of them much madder than his. His followers worried me though,
pressing in around me they formed a menacing circle that I didn't

quite know what to do about. By now the hounds were going mad. Foxy was getting away and they were losing the scent. Jumping down, the red-coated figure with the sergeant-major moustache waggled his crop at me. 'How dare you, sir, interfere with our hunt!—Stand aside at once.' I felt obliged to retreat. 'I'm not stopping you; how was I to know where you wanted to go.' A hard-faced bitch rode nearer to me, 'You should be horse-whipped, you impudent young devil.' Feeling more alarmed now I hastily quit my defence of the gate and let them through. Though now they were only trotting. They knew they would never get Brer Fox that day. I heard one of them say 'I've a good mind to set the hounds after that idiot.'

That night I tossed and turned but couldn't put the event out of my mind. Then suddenly I found myself in the hallway of a great castle. I was dressed in a great scarlet coat and riding breeches. I was attended by two liveried servants who wore jockey caps. Each of them carried a trumpet which they now lifted to their lips and drove out a great blast. At once people in all shapes and sizes streamed out, and stood under me. They turned white, supplicant faces up and then I saw who they were. First there were the people I had seen that morning led by their master. Then there was a ragged, tatty bullfighter whose memoirs I had just finished reading in a Sunday paper. Beside him were two raddled old witches of women who loved cockfighting. At first I was perplexed and didn't know what to say or do. All I could hear from the throng were low moans of *mercy, oh great master of the hunt, mercy on us.* Annoyed, I was turning to go away when the two servants blew another blast to silence them and handed me a great long scroll. Throwing my voice out over them, I read like notes of doom: 'Punishment for all those perverted creatures who have harried, cut and torn to pieces innocent creatures whose only crime was that they were defenceless.' Then from across the hall came a grisly procession of torn and mangled animals. First there came a stag, his great head lowered by the weight of two hounds, whose teeth were sunk into his throat. Then a fox, his sightless eyes lifted up to the sky as he was lifted up again and again, and rubbed into the face of a weeping child. Then came a lioness, lying on her back, her life's blood spilling down her great jaws while three little cubs in bewilderment yelped and pawed at her to play with them. Almost mad with temper I searched for any sign of sorrow in the killers.

There was none, only fear as to what might happen to them. The old master of the hunt just leaned forward on his shooting stick and sneered. In a voice like thunder I roared, 'You are not fit to live, none of you, but yet you must have the same chance as the animals.' Pointing to the master I said, 'You, my bold sir, prepare yourself for tomorrow morning. You will leave that gate, and within ten minutes my hounds will be after you.' I pointed down to a cellar where through an iron grating he could see the hounds all leaping up and snapping the air with their great jaws. Sneering, he replied, 'I won't be a party to your silly game. I'll stay here, and you can kill me on the spot.'

I smiled. 'Oh no you won't. When we turn you loose like the fox you will run till you die.' Then I turned to the bullfighter. 'You, my friend, must come with me now. We have another bull for you to fight, only this time it will be a real bull fight. Just you and the bull.' Shivering, he wrapped his silly cloak around his shoulders and walked after me. Just outside the castle was an arena. Into it came a bull, but not the sort he had seen in Spain. This one was a prize three-year-old, as tall as the side of a house and with mountainous shoulders. He had a wide, massive head, and from his nose there dangled a long chain flecked with blood. Above in the stands some donkeys, hens and foxes sat flapping their wings and banging their tails, while the donkeys brayed and brayed like women screaming. Terrified, the bullfighter let his cloak fall to the ground and turned back from the mouth of the pit. Two pike men barred his way. 'Go now and fight a real bull for a change,' I ordered. Inside the ring the bull pawed furtively at the ground and swinging his great head from side to side threshed the dirt with his chain. Desperately the man ran for the far side of the arena, but tripped over his spindly sword. Half sitting, he turned to look up at the heavy snorting of the bull as he charged straight for him. Half choked with terror he raised his hands in a useless attempt to ward off the tearing, gouging horns. After rolling him the way a sausage is rolled with a fork, the bull knelt down and pressed the ragged bundle of pulpy cloth into the ground. Up above, the animals' cheer was brought to a shrieking crescendo by a cock, who screamed his heart out with delight.

Next morning I walked to the door with the master of the hunt. Defiant, he just smiled thinly as I pulled back the heavy steel-shod door and let him go. Down below, the barking of the dogs became more and more excited as they realised the hunt was on. He had no sooner cleared the fields and dived into the woods than I slipped the bolt and sent them in a long, baying line after him. I returned to the hall and told the rest of the weeping women and white-faced men, 'Your time is nigh. Get ready for the morrow.' All the day I heard the cry of the hounds in the distance, then it grew fainter until it faded away altogether. Weary I went to my bed and lay down to sleep . . .

Then from the window came a scratching noise. I started up to look in the face of the hunt master. 'But,' I stuttered, 'the hounds. I thought . . . ' In one hand he held a dead hound by the scruff of the neck. Flinging it straight at me he cried, 'They're all dead, do you hear, all dead, and there, my idiot friend, is the last of your blasted hounds.'

'But how did you do it?' I cried.

He grinned, 'Aha, and that is where you miscalculated man's ingenuity. Some I led to the river and drowned. Some I raced over a ravine and let them hurtle to the ground fifty feet below. The rest I killed with this.' He shoved forward the branch of a tree, whittled down to a knife point. 'You see,' he continued, 'man is superior after all. It is this that gives us the right to hunt what we damn well please, even a miserable specimen like you.' Cowering back, I screamed and screamed as he advanced, aiming the spear at my belly.

When I awoke I felt a thrill of delight run over me that I was alive and well.

Part II

Part II

CHAPTER FOURTEEN

The Land Across the Sea

*The ship set sail in a manner of speaking
but sure it was only the engine creaking.*

FOR HUNDREDS of years prime cattle and mature men have been Ireland's chief export to England. The old Irish song tells us to—

'Go seek your fortune darlin' in the land across the
sea for in Paddy's land but poverty you'll find.'

But then, no young man or woman is sorry to go. The only ones I ever saw weeping were those left behind. I walked up the gangway, quite elated at the thought of pastures new. First I roamed the ship, taking in all its power and majesty. It was the biggest boat I had ever seen, let alone been on. I looked round its big saloon with its little groups of passengers, all sitting round quietly as though they were in church. Already some of the idiots were making for the bar, glad at least that they should always have the pub with them. It was evening as I stood on the deck looking back to land. All round the hills little pinpoints of light came on, here, there and everywhere, like pins in a pin-cushion. I tried to feel sad that I was leaving my haunts behind, but I didn't, and then I felt ashamed because I didn't. Then I got fed up feeling ashamed and wished to Christ that the bloody boat would push off and let me get to hell out of here. I had a travelling companion. Small and English-looking he yet headed the Irish committee of the Communist Party. He got this post mainly because, like all small men, he wanted power, no matter how strange a figure he would cut at St. Patrick's Night dances, clad in his kilt and great Celtic brooch. He became more Irish than the Irish themselves. Still, he had the good manners to book a bunk for me, and when I got tired of looking at the unending green sea, I just went down below and had myself a feed of black and white pudding. Suddenly I heard the engine change down a

95

note or two, and sure enough, the grey heap called Holyhead hove into view.

I was appalled at the sight of the Welsh-British railwaymen. They looked poor, and even worse, hard-working. In fact, they seemed to be the very same excited 'every-man-a-boss' gang that I had left behind in Dublin. I had never associated England with mundane, poorly paid work. I had regaled myself with legendary tales of ordinary men who had saved thousands while doing little or nothing on bomb-damage repairs. All this looked like grim unexcitable toil. Then I had to file through the customs. A short immaculate looking man bearded me with an 'Anything to declare,' and shoved a card at the bottom of which I was to be sure that I fully understood all things customs-wise under pain of dire penalties.

I answered brightly: 'No, I have nothing to declare, except . . .' His eyes darted at me, '. . . except a pound of black and white pudding.'

My little joke, coming as it did at half-past four in the morning, didn't seem to appeal to his sense of humour. Angrily waving his notice board, he demanded a look at the contents of my case. It was a large brown one bound up with rope. I wouldn't have taken it at all, but it was the only one I had and I had to have something to carry my black and white pudding in. Impatiently he rapped the counter with his bit of cardboard as I wrestled with the rope. Finally I got it off and tipped up the lid. For a full minute he gazed down into my box, empty save for a pair of extremely smelly socks. With an amused contemptuous grin he hoisted them aloft on the end of his board and said, 'Is this really all you have?' Annoyed at him, trying to make me look a fool, I replied, 'Yes. Is there any law against it. That's all I have. I don't know what I should declare about them except they need a good wash.' My next inspection came from the Special Branch detectives, who picked me up just after I passed their box. One of them, a tall, thin, square-looking man, said; 'Behan, Behan, ah now, and how is Brother Brendan getting on?' Flattered by his interest I said, knowingly, 'He's fine. The last I heard of him he was smuggling on Dutch boats.' Bringing his lips back against his teeth like a dog he mused, 'Dutch boats. Ah, he's a lad, ain't he? Still, better for him to be persecuting the Dutch and leave us alone for a while, eh?' I gave him the standard nod you give to all authority. 'Righto then, Brian, is it,' he checked my permit, 'run along now or you'll miss your train.'

Meanwhile my travelling companion had vanished down the far end of the train. Later I taxed him with this, pointing out that he should have remained nearby as I might have been in real trouble. His reply was to the effect that a man in his position, travelling back and forth on revolutionary business, couldn't afford to get into trouble. As our train rolled on and on I thought it would never stop. I thought I was going to the North Pole, not London. Then we rolled through Crewe. To me, accustomed to railway stations with two or three lines at the most, to see a hundred stretch out with lamps lighting them like streets in a town was staggering.

Eventually, tired and weary, we arrived at Euston. My companion, without asking me where I had to go or whether I had enough on me for a cup of tea, bade me farewell. Just before he went he reminded me that I owed him for the berth. Out of six shillings and eightpence, I thrust three and fourpence into his paw.

That first day I spent with the pigeons in Leicester Square. Then, like Shakespeare's Antonio, I hied me to the Elephant, there to lodge. The Elephant is guarded at each end by the two vast lodging houses, Lord Rowton's at Newington Butts, and The Sally Ann at Waterloo Road. At the Rowton I couldn't get in because it was booked out. Sadly I made my way to the Salvo. There I could get a bed in the open dormitory for a shilling. It's a pretty rough old lodging house, this, and the men of God employ extremely un-godlike chucker-outs to deal with the drunks that roll round hammering on the door for admission after lights out. One night I saw the boxer in action. He just waited until the drunk had reached the highest crescendo of noise, then he opened the little trap door suddenly, and let go a right hander like the spring coming up out of a jack-in-the box. The drunk got the message. Most of the tramps there I found to be mean, dirty and objectionable. Certainly they hated the sight of each other, and it was more than you dared to let anyone know you possessed anything more than twopence. On my first night I wondered whether they were all cripples I was sleeping with. I couldn't see a shoe anywhere. Then I saw it. They had stuck the iron legs of the bed down on the shoes to prevent their fellow men from robbing them.

The next morning when I was washing myself, I chanced to look up into the mirror. There was a man walking away with what I was certain was my jacket. Running after him, I pointed out that it was, in fact, my jacket. He just grinned and said, 'Oh, is it,' and handed it back to me. I was advised by the older inhabitants that I should make my way to see my Uncle Nab in order that I could get financial aid.

The clerk who interviewed me was an Irishman.

'How long are you over here?' he queried.

'Two days.'

At this he looked up. 'Two days? Well it didn't take you long to find your way here.'

Resenting the innuendo I said tartly, 'Well, if it didn't take me long I'm still a cheaper bet than you. I'm only over here two days, you must be here at least twenty years.'

The Assistance Board wouldn't give me any money, but instead made out a voucher which covered me for a week with my Sally Ann.

Still, it was much better than some of the digs I was to run into later. Disgusting holes, where, in one, a woman told me she couldn't put sheets or blankets on the bed till I paid her the money in rent, so that she could go out and buy them. In another, I crept down a bit early to find an old rascal peeing in the sink with one hand, while he turned our sausages over the pan with the other. I shouted sourly at him, 'Mind you don't get mixed up, there.'

CHAPTER FIFTEEN

Two Cities for the Price of One

I WASN'T long in the Salvation Army Hostel when I got an invitation to spend the Christmas with some friends of mine in the North country. It was warm and friendly in the train as we slipped up north. I had two Americans to share the carriage with me. Sailors back from South America, their ship had docked into London and they were tripping up to Manchester to share their Christmas with some women.

To my horror they whipped out a deck of cards and invited me to have a game. Like Little Dorrit's father I would beg, borrow, steal or plunder so long as I could have a place at the table. The very sight of cards sets up a wave of tingling excitement all over me that blinds me to anything else. Like all Yanks they looked purse proud. Dressed in heavy macaw jackets, they were rhiny with big heavy gold wristwatches. To keep the company's hearts up they had a large bottle of rum, which they passed round as though it were water. A smooth man on my left agreed to make up the four needed to give the school a bit of life. He was a small, neat man, a buyer for a Leeds clothing firm. As the train swayed and wrestled with mile after mile of track, the pot grew bigger and bigger. Now pound notes were sticking up out of a heap of silver like seed packets in a garden. Try as we would, we could not get the game going. We went from a pair of jacks to open right up to aces, and back again, without anyone at the right time having the pair we needed. Then one of the Yanks smiled. He was a big round man, shaped like a milk bottle. 'Wal, I reckon I'll let her go for, lemme see now, half the pot. That's what we said our opening bet was to be, didn't we. Well then, I make it four pounds for you people to play with me this time.'

My heart sank. Four quid. I hadn't four pence—everything I had was there in the pot. I got ready to sling my hand in. As I picked up I saw a flash of red. Unbelievably I looked again. Not a black one to be seen. Just five glowing red cards. I could feel my heart thump wildly.

I was holding the four, five, six, seven and eight of diamonds. A running tipped flush, one of the best hands in draw poker. I began to go hot and cold in fits. I could feel my whole body squeeze up with excitement. Taking out my wallet I flipped back the corners of half a dozen fivers, and said to the Yank, 'Right. I'm in. You'll have to beat this lot till I get myself sorted out.'

Mightily impressed, he waved his hand. 'Take your time, Briney Boy, we trust you.'

Little did they know that all they were looking at was the corners of fivers pasted on to a square piece of cardboard. The rest of the fivers were long since spent, and all I had left was six triangular pieces cut off each one. At once the Yank folded. 'Too strong for me, you old carpet bagger, this sure is your lucky night.'

Looking across at him I said, 'Well, I might as well be a poor man as a poor boy. I'll see your twelve and raise you twelve. That makes it twenty-four quid in all.' I reached into my wallet and started making fake mental calculations aloud as to how much I'd have left out of thirty quid. For a full minute the Leeds man hesitated. 'Twenty-four quid, boy you must be strong.'

The Yank, eager to get on into another game, said, 'Come on, Mac, quit preaching. Put up or shut up.'

'I wonder, should I . . .' Looking at me he tapped the top of his cards.

'Do what you like,' I said. 'It's your money.'

Pulling his lips back across his teeth he twisted his mouth in defeat. 'No, I don't think I will, no sense in throwing good money after bad.' Stroking his chin with the cards he suddenly passed them on top of the pot. 'No, it's too rich for my blood, Pat, still, do you mind if I take a look at what beat me?' Reaching out to take in the money I blocked his hand with my elbow. 'I do mind, as a matter of fact—you wouldn't pay to see them, so why should I show you them for nothing.' To rub the dirt into the wound, I said, 'You can have a look, Yank, if you want to.'

Eagerly he picked up my cards. 'Well, I'll be buggered by a jackass. By god, my old Briney, you went the limit on a broken flush.'

'Where?' I said violently.

Slowly he spread my cards out face upwards. They were all the one colour, but not the same kind. In my excitement I had mistaken a heart for a diamond. And my heart wasn't the six needed to complete

the run, it was the nine. My stomach turned over, and I hurried down
the corridor to the bog. Standing and swaying with the roll of the train,
I got quietly sick into the wash basin.

The train rolled into London Bridge, and I was busy trying to make
out where the city of Manchester ended, and the city of Salford began.
To this day I am not sure.

Manchester I found to be a happy, prosperous town. I have never
felt so much at home anywhere before or since. The place I was staying
in, Moss Side, seemed to be all Irish and Blacks. My host was a plas-
terer named John Fitzroy. Tall and slim, with black hair, he looked
about the most intellectual worker you could meet. He had a quick,
nervous way of talking that inevitably ended up in a semi-girlish giggle.
He had five sisters, a tame mother, and a father who only showed any
emotion after the twenty-fifth pint of wallop.

The first thing Fitzroy did was to take me on a drinking tour of the
town. We started off and wandered on to a bombed site that serves as a
meeting place for all advanced Mancunians. Here a very bearded
member of the local secular society was busy lampooning God. In a
series of old prints he showed the Bible saying that, 'Man was created
in the image of God.' 'Well, look here,' he shouted. 'The Bible says that
God made man to his own likeness. Well look, here is primeval man.'

Peeping out of a cave was one of the most loathsome faces I have
ever seen. It had a large hand of hair reaching down over a half ape-like
face. In his hand he held a club to match the howling snarls that were
emerging from his slime-encrusted jaws. Striking the picture a whack,
the man tried to drive his point home.'Is this, then, the likeness of your
God? Well, if it is, isn't he a lovely sight? What an intelligent God he
looks, don't he? Well, if this is your creator I am happy he isn't mine.'

Impressed, I walked on, marvelling that such a heathen could live
and breathe. I knew that in Dublin he wouldn't have lasted long before
they threw him into the Liffey.

As the evening wore on I got drunker and drunker. Out at Barton
Bridge I stood and pondered the miracle of the canal flowing fifteen
feet above the road. When ships want to pass they simply twist the
bridge round out of the way, first shutting off the water with steel
locks, leaving trickles of water running down its ends. When the boats
have passed they turn it back again, with its suspended weight of tons

of the old *aqua pura*. Out at Trafford Park I saw the miles of giant engineering plants that make this city one of the steel centres of Britain. I stood in the half light of a warehouse and watched the huge magne-tised crane pick up 100-foot girders and stack them neatly one on top of the other.

Back in town we drank steadily on till I didn't know whether it was Christmas day or Easter. We were just going by a pub, when I heard a scream. Fitzroy seemed to recognise the voice. 'That's my sister,' he exclaimed. Away he went straight through the swing doors. As he didn't come out, I became a little alarmed, and went in after him. He was there all right, lying right in the centre of the floor on the flat of his back. As I helped him outside, he was half-crying from vexation. 'It was my sister, Brian. That fella, Smith, tried to put his hand up her clothes. I told him off about it and he landed me one.' In my drunken-ness I was most distressed at my poor mate lying there on the ground. Running back to the door I called upon this Smith, whoever he was, to come out and try to knock me down. By now a crowd of shoppers had gathered, including some Dublin men. Delighted to see a fight about to commence they drew a ring round me. Feeling very pleased with myself at being the centre of attraction, and seeing no sign of Smith, I became even more daring. I threw off my jacket and started to jump on it. 'By God,' I shouted, 'if that animal, Smith, ever does come out may the Lord look down on him, because I will leave him in gores of blood.' My supporters grew frenzied at this, and one of them declared, 'By God, you're the heart's blood of a Dublin man, so ye are. By God, you would bate that Smith with your cap.'

Then to my anguish Smith appeared. Looking at him I thought I must have been mad to have been shouting so loud. Black-haired, he was one of those Spanish-looking, West of Ireland men. His mother must have been crossed with a shire horse, by the arms he swung at me. He wore a loose suit, with wide shoulders, only his weren't padded. Although it was a bitter cold December day his shirt was bared to the navel. At once I knew discretion would be the better part of valour. Twisting, I tried to make my way through the crowd, muttering as I went, 'So he hadn't the guts to come out.' Two of my supporters seized my arms. 'There he is, Ginger, Ah sure, he's no match for the likes of you. You'd bate two of his kind any day of the week.'

Turning back, I decided on a propaganda war. Roaring and screaming, and pretending to foam at the mouth. 'Hold me back, or by the
living God above me I'll be dug out of him.'

Unfortunately, no one held me back, and I was left roaring away.
Whatever about my appearance, my roaring certainly seemed to have
an effect on him. As I ranted on, spilling tubs of blood with my tongue,
he became more and more interested in what I was saying. Emboldened, I rushed at him and to my undying surprise he turned his back
on me, and I half-shoved, half-pushed him. Feeling I was carrying
matters too far he swung his fist, and drove me from one side of the
crowd to the other. Then to my joy I heard one of my followers warn,
'Run for it, Dublin. It's the police.'

Gratefully I let myself be led away, protesting loudly at the same
time for the benefit of the faithful, that when I got loose I would
mangleise Smith. The policeman who had me was young and nervous.
Nervous, because our way lay through some gas-lit alleys, and doubtless, after hearing and seeing my wild war-dance against Smith. Un-
doubtedly it would have frightened the wild Fuzzy Wuzzy, let alone
a nineteen-year-old cop. So I halted there and then and looked him
straight in the eye.

'Now, constable; you know, and I know, that I was not the cause
of that row. So why should you take an innocent man in. Look, I'm
going back to London tomorrow night, and I won't see this place
any more.'

At first he wouldn't hear of it. But as I refused to go any further,
and he was now going to have to face the worst propaganda since the
mongols, he relented. In as gruff a voice as he could manage he told
me to, 'Buzz off now, and don't let me catch you round the Alex again.'

My poor mate, Fitzroy, came out of the station, black and blue.
Looking at his plastered face, his mother said, 'Ah, me poor boy,
you're the lavings of batings. The dirty things, to do that to any poor
mother's son.'

That night, John and I took a slow walk down to the dance hall. On
the way down, he said, 'Do you know who that was you were fighting?

Feeling easy in my mind, I replied, 'I neither know nor care.'

'Well, you should care. He's the local tearaway. He's just done
three years for causing bodily harm.'

Sweating profusely, I handed my coat in at the cloak room. Inside, the band was playing soft, sweet music, while the great speckled ball shot shafts of magical light round the darkened hall. Suddenly, the band stopped, and the spell was broken. Heads came up off dreamy shoulders, and the couples reluctantly disengaged and walked back to the side.

Then I saw, coming straight at me, Smith, surrounded by at least a dozen equally savage-looking henchmen. I looked round to see what door was nearest, but then there he was, grinning, and holding out his hand. 'No hard feeling, Dub. That was a great fight last night.' Turning to his long locked cronies he said,

'And Billy Smith isn't the man to bear a grudge. Right boys?'

Feebly I shook his hand and went off with him for a celebration drink.

When the train reached Blackfriars on my return, it seemed as though I had been away years, not two weeks. Just as I was coming across the Blackfriars bridge I was met by a bum. A Scotch man, he said, 'Look, Pat, give us the price of me kip.' I was going to reach into my pocket to befriend him when I got a whiff of whisky. He was drunk, and doubtless intended to drink mine as well. I brushed him to one side and went on.

I was no sooner back in London when I walked up Farringdon Road. I wanted to see the *Daily Worker* building. To us in Ireland, this was our local Kremlin, our temple. An embattled workers' press, fighting daily for survival. In fact, I thought it looked a bit dingy. Then I made every effort to join the Communist Party. It seemed to me that the enemies of the Catholic Church, whom I linked with poverty and oppression, must be my friends. But I had no success. The local party branch, as with most working-class areas, simply didn't exist. It is further north in Hampstead that London's Red Belt lies.

Then one day I was walking past the Festival of Britain site. Outside, a Communist speaker blared away at the workers on the site. Delighted, I asked one of the stewards for an application form to join the party. The speaker, seizing my completed form, waved it aloft triumphantly. 'It gives me great pleasure to tell you that one of your fellow workers has decided to join our glorious party, vanguard organisation of the working-class. I hope that many of you will follow his example.'

It was 1950, and I was a member of the British Communist Party.

CHAPTER SIXTEEN

The Gold Fever

'I want,' I said to the girl, 'a cup of tea, and two slices of toast.'

The cafe was small and dark, cowering, half hidden, under a great railway bridge. Yet it seemed a gay, hearty place. It was full of cheerful rich market porters. An Englishman's club is the café. There, surrounded by mighty pillars of bacon and egg, he can escape the drudgery of his hours.

Hesitantly, I offered the girl my two bob, and sat down. Opposite me sat two of the market men, laughing and jostling with each other. With their big leather aprons they looked proud, defiant, a breed apart. Of course, they are, too. To fetch, lift and carry sides of beef, or sacks of spuds, you need a strong back, and the agility of a cat. When my mountain of toast came, they both smiled.

'You off your grub then, Pat,' cracked one.

'He don't like bread,' followed up the other.

At first I felt embarrassed, then annoyed. What had it to do with them what I ate. Even worse, how did they know I was a Paddy. I had said nothing to them. It made me feel as though I carried some scar or mark that stamped me 'Made in Bogland.' And yet there was no malice in them.

Just opposite the café was a church. Derelict and gaunt, it was squat and square like a warehouse. For pure ugliness it would have been hard to beat. Outside it had a chart like a thermometer showing the amounts donated to rebuild it.

'How much have you put in the box, Alf?' said the fat one.

'Nothing mate. They've got a sight more than me. It's all a bleedin' racket, ain't it, Pat?'

I just nodded dumbly. Coming from Ireland, a land awash with prayer, this sort of talk knocked me cold.

'You a Catholic, Pat?' I nodded again. 'Well then, you should know what a racket all this religion is. Look at your country. You'd think with all the praying that's done over it, it'd be a land of milk and honey. But it ain't. It's in a worse state than China, where they don't do any praying at all. Naw, it stands to reason, praying never did no one any good.'

If I had to pray for anything just then it would have been for the meat and two veg that I couldn't afford. The little café girl was lashing out with the college pudding, a lovely round sweet with custard trickling down its spicy flanks. Slowly, my pile of toast dwindled. Nearer and nearer came the moment when I must rise and face work again. My toast-eating activities had been brought on by an acute shortage of cash. I had been forced to put the arm on my ganger for the loan of two bob.

I was working in one of the dreariest parts of London—historic Southwark. My place was one of those endless lines of factories and warehouses that bar the river bank from London Bridge to Blackfriars. It seems a shame that a noble river bank should be ruined when really there is no need. The factories are no longer fed exclusively by the river. Maybe some day, Morris's dream of a Fairyland Thames, dedicated to pleasure, will come true. I could hardly have looked for a more filthy job. But then they had a twelve-hour shift, six-day week, and I certainly needed the money. Still, my work had a certain element of romance. We were pile drivers. The essence of pile-driving is that you twist thirty-foot long pencils of earth out of the ground. In its place you ram down a solid core of concrete. Dot this round the place and you have a raft to float your building on. Our building wasn't a very big one, but the ground was bad, hence the piles. Being the month of December the site was like a swamp. As we tried to turn length after length of tubing down we staggered and floundered about like ducks on a muddy bank. My fellow men were nearly all regulars with the firm. There were only four or five casuals like me.

I got to know this when I tried to sound them out about joining the union. They just didn't want to know. I tried chatting a few of them up at tea break, but, while they would listen, they weren't going to do anything to put them in queer street with the firm.

I had two mates, one a Scotsman, the other from the North of Ireland. Both of them were semi-skilled. They had to be able to operate the rig and keep it mobile. The Scotsman was middle aged and had had some experience of unions. He lacked the simple faith of the unskilled in unions or leaders. 'Now look here, Pat,' he said, 'you're all right, but you're not the union. They don't give a damn about us. Once they get to the top that's it. I was a union man, but I got fed up with it. There's no future in it, not for you or me. You have to look out for number one. No, I wouldn't join nothing. I won't even join my hands in prayer.'

The North of Ireland man was medium sized, black haired and broad. He just listened to me and smiled good naturedly. Still, I kept on at it. What prodded me was the appalling mud that caked your hands and splashed all over you. Naturally, there was nowhere to wash. The best you could do at the end of the day was to get a bucket of hot water out of the compressors and wash in that. We started at 7.30 in the morning, and went on till 7.30 at night. We finished as we started by the light of flares. Then it was cold. My God, how cold it was. I smoked fag after fag, more to keep myself warm than anything else. Every now and again trains stopped over our heads. I spent my time envying the watchers gazing down from a nice, warm carriage. I wondered where they were going, what they were doing. Occasionally, a Continental wagon rolled up with large mysterious letters 'Belgium' written all over it.

To add to my torments I couldn't even sleep in my digs. An old kip-house in the Blackfriars Road, we slept six to a room. To dress you literally had to climb up on top of your bed. You couldn't find room on the floor. It was cold in our basement, but it was colder still in the room at the back of ours. One night we were all awakened to the sound of a man running like mad round and round the room. Fearful, we went in, and there was the backroom lodger, fully clothed, jumping up and down like a maniac. Frantically, he pointed to the ceiling. 'By God, if I don't get warm soon, I am going up there to throw her fancy man out of her rattle pit, and jump in myself.' The last I ever saw of him he was making for a bus going over Blackfriars Bridge. As he caught it he turned and said, 'I will get warm digs, see if I don't.'

Our landlady was an ex-prostitute. Not the rounded breasty type that excites you in the columns of the Sunday press. She was the real thing. Endless degradation by men had sharpened her hatchet face to a razor edge. Ruthlessly she had scraped the last vestige of hair from over her eyes. In their place ran black daubs that made her look like the wicked queen in Walt Disney's 'Snow White'. She was always on about her daughter. 'She's a good girl, Mr Behan. I hope you won't allow any of the others to take liberties with her.' She was forever pestering me to know if this fellow or that was out to despoil her Linda. Looking at Linda I could see why her mother had gone on the streets. Tall, thin and gangly, she had the added affliction of being coldly stupid. Like her mother, she hated the lodgers, believing they were several cuts below her. Every time she brought in the dinner she would avoid smiling and simply put the dinner down, as though it was nothing to do with her.

One day, weary and mudstained, I opened the door and was just going down below when the landlady's door opened and she collared me.

'Mr Behan,' she said, 'you must help me. I am convinced there's something going on between Mr Middleton and my Linda.' I stared in disbelief. Mr Middleton was an ex-Japanese P.o.W. While he looked nigh unto death, he seemed to be always flush. 'That man's a ponce, Mr Behan, nothing more or less than a dirty ponce, and I don't want my Linda getting mixed up with him.'

That night I took a closer look at him. He seemed the poor ponce type. Weak and shabbily dressed, someone even the lowest pro could feel superior, if not equal, to. The following night she came at Middleton. By now he was getting browned off with the whole affair.

'Mr Middleton,' she started.

'Look, Mrs Bartle. I know nothing at all about your daughter, and I care less.'

'Oh, that's a fine way to talk, I must say.'

'All I want is my dinner.' He could get the smell of it, and even more ominous behind her the hungry lodgers were making for the dining room. This was serious, because in a minute the lodgers would genteelly sweep the two plates of bread clean. Still she kept on nattering. Finally, almost mad with hunger he burst out: 'Your Linda would be as safe as houses in a monastery full of randy monks. And if you want the plain, uncoloured truth, I wouldn't piss on her if she was on fire.' With that he shot into the dining room, only to see the last of the bread disappear.

In the meantime, the job was getting no better. Until, one day, our lead pile started to bounce off something hard. Try as we would we couldn't get it to go down one inch further. Our ganger was most annoyed. Paid by results, he didn't want any hanging about. Pointing down the hole he said, 'Hop down there, Pat, and see what it is.'

I gave the obstruction a rap of a pick, but nothing stirred. 'Must be a rock of some sort,' I shouted up.

'Here, then, try this on it.' He lowered down a pneumatic drill, and I started blasting away. After a couple of seconds a long piece of metal came away under the drill. My ganger, interested, called down:

'Let's have a look at that, Pat.' Picking it up he went off into a huddle with a scrap merchant, who called on our site every day. Ostensibly looking for old cast pipes, or lengths of lead, he was capable of whipping anything that moved. Usually, builders discourage them. One general foreman told a totter he had some scrap. Unfortunately, stacked underneath the scrap, were fifty new wash basins. Later, in court, the totter said he thought that when the general pointed over 'there' he meant 'All that was a lying there.'

Our totter wore a black hat and white scarf; he pushed one of those long, boat-shaped barrows. From where I was I could see he was getting excited, gabbling away to beat the band, and pointing over to our hole. Our ganger then strolled back, casually, and looked down. 'Now, Pat, any more of that old stuff you find, just put it on one side for your old uncle Wally.' There are times in the affairs of men, and I decided this was one of mine. 'Well, Wall, I don't really know if I should do that.'

Leaning forward, he said, 'Wouldn't like to do what, me old Pat?'

'Anything criminal, Wall. All of my family are very respectable. We have never had any trouble with the police.'

'Whatever are you on about, Pat. Who said anything about the police?'

'Well then, if it's all right with you, Wall, I will just pop out and ring the head office of the firm, and tell them what I have found. I know that everything we dig up belongs to either them or the client we build for.'

Pushing his hat back, he said, admiringly, 'You're not daft, Pat, are you. But we don't want to worry the head office about a little thing like this.'

'Little,' exclaimed Jock. 'There must be a ton of lead down there.'

'And,' chimed in the North of Ireland boy, 'bluey is now a fiver a hundredweight.'

Lowering his voice, the ganger took command. 'Now lads, let this be our little secret. You chaps can help me, and I can help you. All you have to do is to dig the stuff out, and I will get rid of it.'

At this the bluey merchant sidled up and started peeping down the hole.

Savagely the ganger rebuffed him. 'Now now, you clown. Do you want to see us all in nick. Come back in the dinner hour.'

Standing in that hole I thought this must be how the gold prospectors must have felt in the Yukon. Alternate waves of elation and depression swept over me.

Then I became suspicious of the other workers. I started to glare balefully at men I had tried to win for the brotherhood of labour not ten minutes before. Two of my erstwhile brothers were working quite near me digging a trench. I was delighted to see they were meeting nothing more exciting than stones and old clay pipes. Apparently our seam ran just ahead of us in larger layers. Being a bombed-out printing works it must have been the lead used by them that we were digging out. It was mine, all mine. Then those two bastards started to get nosy. As fast as I tossed the stuff up to Jock, so they tried to get a squint before he shoved it into a sack. Unable to control their curiosity any longer they made as if to come and look at what we were doing. Immediately, I felt a hot wave of anger sweep over me. 'Poky swine,' I thought, 'they can ruin everything.'

One of them smiled at me. I screwed my face up at him in reply. 'What's the matter with you, then, Pat?' called one of them.

'Nothing,' I said, 'Nothing at all. We have our work to do here and it would answer you better to get on with yours.'

'Huh, you can go off people you know.'

At this, Jock joined in. 'You can go off who you like, mate, but leave us alone.'

Delightedly I watched the two of them slink back in their hole.

At dinner hour our totter came back. Furtively, we loaded eight sacks into the belly of his barrow. Throwing an old raincoat over them he started to move away. For a slight man, he was inspired with the strength of ten. When I went to help he pushed me away with, 'I will manage all right, Pat. I'll manage.' And he did.

That night my landlady had her revenge for my rudeness. I was to be transported to the top floor. The penalties were obvious. More stairs to climb. Four flights to the washhouse and lavatory. Not that the latter worried my room-mates. One of the dirty animals proceeded to pee into a brown paper bag before my very eyes. 'Well, here goes nothing,' said he, tossing it out the window.

Whether my new room-mates were trying to impress me or not I couldn't say, but no sooner had I gone to bed than I spotted one vile bandit cautiously lift up the window and commence to pee. As there was a very strong wind blowing straight back at me I protested very loudly indeed. All to no avail. The rude creature simply laughed and said, 'Well, Ginger, you have learned tonight that the only way to get your own back in this life is to pee against the wind.'

Revolted, I determined at once to seek pastures new. I had no sooner put my head down to sleep when I heard a noise like thunder. Alarmed, I inspected the wretches, but they all lay quiet enough. Then the noise seemed to get closer until our door was flung open, and there stood a policeman, breathing fire and fury.

'What dirty cow son did this?' he roared. 'This' was his cape drenched in some foul smelling liquid. Getting no answer, he started to prod the sleepers. The man who had thrown the bag out was the sauciest of the lot.

'What do you think you're poking then?' he cried. 'Do you think it's a load of old dossers you have to deal with?' Standing naked except for his shoes, he went on, 'We have our rights, you know, and you should be the last to burst into a room like this.'

Impressed by this lawful type of argument, the bobby came down a note or two, and started to appeal for sympathy against the villain who had thrown water, or something even worse, over his cape. Sensing a weakness, the paperbag one started to cast doubts on the whole story.

'You have to be careful, you know,' he admonished the copper. 'You might be barking up the wrong tree. How do you know, for instance, that you might have not been caught in a sudden shower of rain.'

At this the bobby grew violent again. 'What do you take me for, an idiot is it. Who ever heard of hot rain coming down in brown paper bags?'

We had to bear with some more general abuse, and then he went his way, determined to avoid passing under open windows.

Our site began to look like Mons. In our search for lead we burrowed hither and thither. Vast mounds of earth rose up, shutting our quarter off from the rest of the site. Then one Tuesday morning a hire-car pulled in and nudged its way up to the gate. A chauffeur ushered two men into my ganger's office.

'God,' remarked Jock, 'that's Dixon, our director, and the bloke with him looks like the factory owner. I wonder what they want?'

We hadn't long to wait. Straight over to us they came, picking their way through channels of mud. They spoke loudly as do all important men. Only mean, scabby little creatures walk around with muted tones.

'I was saying to Mr Moore, Browne, that we are up to schedule, isn't that right?'

Our Wally almost bent his head. 'Oh, that's right, sir. Indeed, we are ahead of schedule.'

'Well,' said Dixon, looking at our mountains, 'these chaps certainly seem to be doing well.'

Wally grinned. 'Oh, indeed they are, sir. Never better.'

After each trip our totter took on new plumage. Now, from head to toe, he was dressed to kill. He was offering round fags, beginning with coffin-nails and ending with Players. I was determined to get rid of the job. I didn't feel safe now. We had dug up so much stuff that the hut was beginning to lean up on one end. After sticking a couple of acrows under it, it seemed to right itself. My evil mind kept telling me that the ganger was a villain, and the sooner I got the money the better. So I jacked the job in.

When I went for my money I had thirteen days pay, plus sixty lovely pounds that he peeled over a wad capable of choking a horse. While I was leaving the hut Dixon, the director, reappeared. Stepping

into the hut he was greeted by an effusive Wally. But as Dixon made
to come forward, his end of the hut started to rise with him. I guessed
immediately the acrows outside were slipping, and the slightest weight
leaving Dixon's end was liable to send the whole caboodle down a
twenty-foot hole.

'For Christ's sake stay where you are,' shouted Wally.

'I beg your pardon, Browne,' came back the director, heavily.

'I am sorry, sir, but this hut is out of balance. Behan, shoot out and
tighten up those acrows, will you. It will be all right, sir, never fear.'

'But I have just packed,' said I, laughing. Almost bursting, Wally
made as if to come towards me, and then the hut gave a fearful creak.
Hastily retreating he begged, 'There's a good chap, Behan. Won't take
a minute.' I became panic stricken. If the hut collapsed, out would
spill the bluey, in would come the law, and so the consequence was I
walked as fast as I could, without actually running, down Southwark
Bridge Road.

Feeling flush, I determined to change my clothes from the share out.
I had my eye on a San Francisco zipper jacket, and a bird's eye suit.
In any case I feared that our digs were lousy, and I determined to rid
myself of the old clobber and dust myself throughout with the most
potent D.D.T. I could find.

Making my way to the Old Kent Road I stood outside a chemist's
and pondered. I wanted to kill two birds with the one stone. As well as the
D.D.T. I had to buy some contraceptives to send back to an acquaintance in Ireland. They are, of course, forbidden there, under pain of
much jailing. I am told since that an enterprising Jamaican has made a
fortune smuggling them in, disguised as religious tracts. My problem
now was to buy them from an extremely attractive young lady, who
looked as though the very mention of either would embarrass her for a
year and a day. But then I thought, 'What prudish nonsense. The girl
is obviously accustomed to this sort of thing.' So bowling in, I went up
to the counter. To my relief, a buxom woman took her place, as she
had to go to the other end. Still slightly embarrassed I said, in a loud
voice, 'Will you please give me six packets of Durex, and a box of your
strongest D.D.T.'

At first she just smiled, then she tittered, then she rocked with
laughter. 'My Lord, tonight, son, you must be doing a line with a very

dirty old bag.' I had to retreat as fast as possible, after telling the woman to serve me and not act the comedian.

Now I had the problem of disposing of my old gear. Never have I found it so hard to get rid of a rolled up bundle before. Every time I went to lob it over a bomb-site wall somebody showed up to stop me. Another problem I faced was that I had inserted in the middle of the bundle a leg of beef that had gone all rotten and hairy. As we were forbidden to cook in the digs I had to get rid of it as best I could. So I took myself down to the banks of the canal that crosses the Old Kent Road, was just going to drop the parcel in the water, when a flashlight blinded me. When I could finally make out the copper behind it, he seemed grim.

'What have you there?' he cried.

'Nothing officer, just some old clothes.'

'Let me see, then.'

I handed the bundle over. Prodding it a few times he suddenly said, 'What's this, then? This doesn't feel like old clothes.'

Despite my protests he shoved his arm in and then went green. 'I have just felt a hairy leg,' he announced to me and the water.

'It's an old leg of beef,' I protested.

'Come along now,' he said, 'Let's not have any trouble.'

Before I knew where I was he had me fast in a judo grip that lasted firm all the way to the station.

CHAPTER SEVENTEEN

Fourteen K.P.R.

KENNINGTON PARK ROAD is one of those roaring traffic lanes that lead out of London to Crawley and Brighton, and other places south. In 1950 I went searching along there for digs. The local Communist Party secretary had his office in the basement of a party member's house, and he had suggested I should try there. It looked an ordinary house. Four storeys and a dusty sycamore in the tiny front garden, and yet, it was to shape my whole future.

The landlord was a Yorkshire man who preached night and day 'If ever tha does owt for nowt, always do it for thy sen.' Fortunately for his innumerable tenants his actions often belied his words. Anyway, he let me and my mate have a nice room, and even more delightful, he had two lovely daughters; one blonde, and one dark. By fortunate chance their bedroom backed onto ours and I could lie on my bed listening to them laughing and giggling as they took their ease.

At this time I was working on the Festival of Britain site, and had in my gang a fellow party member. I got to know he was a Red in this wise.

My gang were mainly Connemara men from the west coast of Ireland. Some of them spoke no English, and none of them had the slightest notion what a trade union was, let alone politics. I used to collect their union dues. They amounted to sevenpence per man per week and the firm allowed me two hours to collect them from seven hundred men. As I went round my gang taking their money, I asked for their cards, so that I could mark them paid. They never had them and if I tackled them about it they just smiled and gave me the money. Then I spoke sharply to them, saying, 'Look here. Bring your cards in with you tomorrow. You know the money's not for me. It's for the union.' They just laughed, showing teeth black to the roots. 'Oh, it's all right, Ginger. We know the money's for you; you must be making a right old haul out of it.' These men were fanatically loyal to people, not things. Me, they liked, and would allow no one to interfere with me.

Once we went on strike, and a labour conciliation officer came on the job to get us to go back to work. He began his speech by telling us that he had come direct from Herbert Morrison to tell us that our stoppages were only injuring the Labour Government, whose show-piece the Festival was. He seemed to be all right with the tradesmen, or some of them, at least, but he failed miserably with the navvies, who could hardly understand what the hell he was blathering about. He had another union official with him who mounted the rostrum to tell us he had very little to add to what Brother Tom had told us. A huge hod-carrier, right up front, then doffed his cap jeeringly and said, 'If you really have nothing to add then what the fucking hell are you doing up there, wasting everybody's time?'

During the meeting I had some words with Tom. To me the Labour Government were nothing more nor less than hungry Tories, and I told him so. During the afternoon some of the lads went out on the beer. In the meantime old Tom had started creeping round the site trying to find a friendly face. He was in fact canvassing the plasterers' steward to get him to move a resumption of work. From round the back of the canteen I heard an agonised wail. It was poor Tom being tugged to and fro between two giant drunken navvies. I rushed to the rescue, much to the surprise of the labourers, who told me they didn't want to listen to any more of his old buck. So these were men with whom you had to tread very lightly. But at the same time, like the elephant, they could easily be worked. For example, though they would knife each other in the pub after a few drinks, a little navvy ganger could make them jump.

Our ganger was a vicious, ignorant pig. He dressed himself up like old Moleskin Joe. He wore a hat, knotted scarf and hard navvy cord trousers. He even chewed tobacco. A swine of the first water. Sooner than leave us alone and unwatched he stood on the top of the trench and pissed where he stood. His signal for the end of the tea break was to pick up a brick and toss it onto the roof of the hut. Yet it never entered any of the navvies' heads to do anything to him. It entered mine, though, and I waited for the day and the hour I could do him an injury.

It was one morning when we were at tea, that my new comrade put his spoke in. One of the navvies asked me if I believed in any religion. Anxious not to hurt their feelings I started to skate and flounder around the question. Then from the corner of the hut a voice came loud and clear. 'It's all balls, is religion. It's just used to deceive us and give the priests an easy living. Can anyone here tell me the last time they saw a skinny parish priest?'

Knowing how the labourers felt about their faith, I half expected these few words to be his last. But nothing happened, and when I got a good look at him I could see why he escaped.

His name was Reilly. In build he was short, like a hairy ape. Not long hair, except on his arms, but short cropped stuff that made him look like Mr Hyde when Jekyll was at his worst. He was, in fact, one of the strongest men in the gang, if not the strongest. In navvy gangs men are always trying to best one another in feats of strength. No two of them could put Reilly down. Once he worked near two bricklayers who were picking up two piers that formed a gate. They had to span the opening by building in a heavy steel girder. It beat the two of them to lift it up onto the top of the piers. Reilly just put his back under it and straightened up, lifting it clean up onto the wall.

He was a worker as well. Like a steam engine he went rooting and tearing up and down a long trench. This was very handy for me, as all I had to do to appear as though I was working was to move up behind him, picking up the little lumps that fell off his shovel. Again, work is the navvy's god, and anyone that was beast for it, like Reilly, they had high regard for. So that, even as they twisted their feet uneasily under the wooden form as they heard their Church assailed, they didn't do anything. Anxious as always to meet a new comrade, that night I invited Reilly to join me in a drink. Sitting across the table from him I could see that the whole of his face was a sore rash under the short hairs that sprouted out in all directions. He looked as ugly an old thing as you could meet in a day's walk.

'Women don't like me, you know.'

'Oh,' I lied, 'I can't really see why not.' May God forgive, I thought, nothing female outside a chimpanzee could possibly find you in the least bit attractive.

'It's me blood,' he announced, starting to pull up his sleeves.

I looked round nervously as those great thunks of flesh appeared. 'But women can't see your blood, surely.'

'No, that's not what I mean,' he shook his head in annoyance. 'It's me blood that makes me break out in all these sores, and it's that what puts the women off me.' Indeed, even right up his arms the pimples were there.

'Well, it must be what you eat. Why don't you get your landlady to do you some salad dinners for a change?'

He scratched his head, perplexedly. 'Sure I have no landlady; I spent last night in the police station. I got mad drunk, and gave me oul landlord a few clouts.'

I hesitated, and then in one of those mad moments of generosity that we spend our lives regretting I made him an offer. 'Well, you know, you're quite welcome to the room with me and my mate. I know he won't object. He's a party member like ourselves.'

So he came to share our room.

My room-mate was a student of economics, called Barry. With his heavy glasses and shock of blond hair he looked as though he was in training to be a professor. I must say he welcomed Reilly with open arms, and at first everything went well. Then one day I came home to a smell that would knock a donkey sideways. In front of an enormous pot, stood Reilly. Into it he was throwing a strange mixture of banana skins, orange peel, and strands of lettuce mixed with carrot tops. He had a peculiar habit of sniffing as he spoke, and his little mean eyes swivelled violently.

'I'm just boiling it up for me blood,' he explained. 'When it's done I'll strain it off and drink the juice of it. You know,' he burst out, 'if I got rid of these sores, some girl might go with me and I wouldn't have to spend my nights in the pub.'

I was surprised at this outburst. He had never hitherto shown any guilt about his drinking, and I suspected that comrade Barry had been lecturing him about wasting his time. But poor old devil, his mind was tormented with loneliness. And yet here and there a flash of peasant suspicion would make him stubborn and argue over a trifle. He had grown to hate my mate Barry. This was mainly because Barry was for-ever reading aloud from heavy economic tomes. Again, he thought Barry was either crackers or showing off, because of the time-table he adhered to rigidly. Pinned up over his bed it proclaimed that he would rise at six, then take a cooling plunge in the open-air swimming pool, follow this by breakfast, and then study. He even had the time he spent talking to us strictly allotted, and at the end of ten minutes would rise abruptly declaring the period at an end.

Reilly's chief complaint against Barry was the long, meaningless jargon-words he used. In the meantime Reilly was casting covetous eyes on the girls in the house, and I resented this. Not just because he coveted all women but because I had my eye on one of the daughters for myself. She was a light-hearted, dark-haired girl just rising seventeen. I was coming up the stairs one day when I met her just leaving her bedroom. She was wearing a tight roll-necked sweater, and her hair was tied back with a blue ribbon. Pretty, yes, but what attracted me most was her cuddly appearance. Here, I felt, was a woman I could squeeze and squeeze to my heart's content. I hate hard, sharp women. They frighten the life out of me and simply make me want to row with them. To deflect Reilly onto other quarry, I suggested he might do worse than call on the single lady who lived on the top floor. She was a middle-aged Irish woman who told everyone that her one great love was shattered when her fiancé was killed in the war, and that she could never love again. Which was fortunate, I thought, for it seemed most unlikely that anyone would be able to love her except perhaps Reilly. She was ugly as sin. Apart from squint eyes, she sported a beard, which made her look like Rasputin's mother. She certainly was no beauty, but then neither was Reilly. I told him she was lonely too, and looking for a mate. The mate part of it was true enough. I inflamed Reilly's heart with tales of how this woman had tried to seduce Barry with the aid of banana sandwiches. Maybe I laid it on a bit. Anyway, he came in that night as drunk as a monkey's uncle and told me he intended to go straight away and plight his troth. Before I could say yea or nay, away he went, carrying as a token, a bag of apples (she too was a vegetarian).

Two minutes later I heard terrible screams coming from upstairs. Dashing up I was joined on the next landing by another tenant, a postman who had only moved in that day, and who looked panic-stricken. He threw open the woman's door only to be thrown bodily out again. Cautiously I kicked open the door and jumped back out of harm's way.

There was poor Reilly, tears streaming down his face. In his out-stretched hand was an apple, but the woman was frightened out of her wits. She was wearing a nightshirt which billowed down to the floor. Pointing to Reilly she shouted, 'Oh Mother a God, get him out of here. Oh the beast, the dirty beast. Attacking a woman in that drunken state.' Alas, poor Reilly, if he'd have gone up sober he'd have been sound. As it was he was kneeling on the floor at our feet blubbering, 'I only wanted to give her an apple.' I took him by the hand and gently led him downstairs.

I soon found that my dark-haired Celia was going out with another fellow. It seemed I couldn't look out of the window but I saw her going off with him, but yet there was a look in her eye that kept me hoping. I used to make up excuses to go down to the kitchen to have a word with her, and whenever I knew she was down there alone, I used to sing 'Shenandoah, I love your daughter,' at the top of my voice. One night she joined in the chorus, and I knew I was home and dry. Luckily for me she was the warm girl I'd thought she was, and we took to each other like ducks to water.

Celia came from a long, long line of atheists and I doubt if she'd even heard of original sin, let alone believed in it.

Back in our room things had reached a stage with Reilly, where he would have to go. He had begun to show his contempt for Barry openly. One day Barry started to go on about how things would be in Ireland once the revolution had begun.

'We shall, of course, eliminate the peasant, that village idiot of rural society.'

At once I detected a murderous glint in peasant Reilly's left eye.

'So,' he muttered, 'you want to get rid of the stupid peasant.'

Barry was delighted at such obvious interest and warmed to his theme. 'But of course, dear chap, that's just it. You must realise that there can be no hope of industrialisation while these country bumpkins are allowed to wander round their loony bins.'

Reilly just kept flexing his muscles and glaring at Barry.

Barry, a little nervous, said, 'Of course, you do understand what I mean when I use the term "eliminate"? '

Reilly shook his bull head and sneered, 'How could I? Aren't I one of your stupid peasants?'

As soon as he was gone Barry trotted over to me. 'Oh dear, I do hope he hasn't got things all wrong. You know when I spoke of "eliminate" I didn't mean physical extermination. My God, no. I simply meant that with mechanisation we would transform the peasant into a farm mechanic.'

However, by that night he seemed to have forgotten all about Reilly, and I had to listen to a long lecture on the merits of celibacy as evinced by the virgin Chinese army. 'They were as fit as fiddles,' he announced. 'Comrade Mao would not tolerate slackers or idlers who wasted their energy on things frivolous.'

I prayed that he might choke or fall asleep. I was anxious to creep in and see Celia. No good, he droned on and on and at last it was I who fell asleep. I was awakened by the sound of a heavy, hobnailed boot crashing the door in. I sprang up to see a drunken Reilly waving a beer bottle in one hand and pointing at Barry with the other.

'Aha, you miserable city bastard. Eliminate the peasant would you? Well, by God, here's one for you to eliminate now, if you're man enough.'

Poor Barry could only blink. Pulling on his glasses he reasoned, 'But look here, my dear chap, this is quite frankly ridiculous. I haven't the slightest wish to wrestle with you in this unseemly way.'

At that, Reilly made a dive at him, swinging the bottle like a club. Terrified, Barry dived between his legs like a startled rat and took refuge under the table. Crouching there, clad only in his jock strap and yellow socks, he squealed in terror.

Laughing cunningly, Reilly brandished his bottle and came after him. 'I'll catch you yet, never fear, and when I do I'll tear your heart out.'

Jumping up, I tried to reason with him, at the same time looking around for a weapon. Giving another of his loony laughs, he tried to push by me. In desperation I grabbed the only thing I could see, his coddle pot, and jammed it down tight over his head. For a moment he staggered around, blinded by the noxious mixture running down his face. Terrible sounds were coming out from under the pot, and I decided to cut and run, when he fell onto Barry's bed and commenced to snore. Poor Barry, too fastidious to use Reilly's bed, spent the night on the floor, muttering over and over, 'Oh, what terrible people.' I don't think he could forgive me for tipping up that horrid pot, even to save his life.

In the basement, our local party secretary was under siege. Our landlord, though a party member himself, believed in a money economy. After losing eighteen months' rent, he decided to shut out God's sunlight from Jacky. Contrary to what you hear, Muscovite gold is nonexistent, at least in the lower ranks of the party, and our secretary had paid no rent since he took up residence. Indeed, he had had no pay in three months. His only reward was escaping work and feeling important as the self-appointed leader of the whole population of Lambeth. Population, two hundred and fifty thousand. As always it was his wife who had to bear the brunt of his boy-man activities. Yet he often told me that he felt he was obeying Lenin's great dictum, and be a 'tribune of the people.' It was a great pity, but the people simply ignored him. No matter how hard we tried, no one would take us and our party seriously. Jack was forever dragging me out to do some silly pathetic, public meeting that no one took the slightest notice of. The only place public meetings are taken seriously is Hyde Park, and the House of Commons, but then, both these have the advantage of being, like the London Palladium, licensed. Once he collared us straight from work, and asked us to man the platform. Really I would have given anything to have gone home, but he looked so pathetic I felt we couldn't leave him to go it alone. Our venue was the back of the Old Vic in a lane just off The Cut, a favourite market place for South Londoners. Standing under a huge, red banner, we roared away for hours, but no one took a blind bit of notice of us. No one, that is, except for a crowd of kids who, using the lid of a dustbin, beat our ears to a frazzle. Then with the aid of a policeman we got rid of them and announced our next speaker, Harry Boaks.

Harry was a 'genuine,' or stage cockney, who went down like a bomb with the intellectual party members, always anxious to hob-nob with a 'real' working man. He was short and broad, with a totally flat face and an eternal cheerful grin, that never faded, not even when his house burnt down killing his ma and his pet budgie. He wore a long jacket and his braces pulled his trousers right up under his armpits His shoes were huge, with three inch rubber soles on which he bounced around, grinning constantly. Because it is so hard to get a real genuine Londoner into the Communist Party he was treated like a crown prince, and his most stupid utterance was greeted with reverent nods.

I called on him to speak, convinced that he alone could get the ear of the cockney toiler. Determined to avoid the usual rubbish about how democratic the party would be once it had seized all power he launched into a vivid description of how terrible things had been for his 'muvver' in the old days. 'Do you know,' he roared, 'my poor muvver never ad a barf.' Startled, a couple of women stopped to look up at him. Looking down, and showering them with drops of spit, he repeated with great emphasis, 'For twenty years my muvver never ad a barf.'

'Cor,' said a voice from behind us, 'she must have bin a dirty old woman, that's all I can say.'

One of the women, no doubt herself a mother, suddenly up and grasping her shopping bag, clouted Harry fair and square round the chops. 'Git down off there,' she shouted. 'You ought to be downright ashamed talking about your mum like that.'

As they turned away, one said to the other, 'Who are they, Ag?'

Looking us up and down, in our rubber boots and cement-spattered donkey jackets, Ag replied, 'I don't know, I'm sure. Out of some old kip house I should say.'

Meanwhile the battle of the basement was hotting up, and secretary Jack was being pushed back and back. The landlord was bunging into that small room every bit of junk he could lay hands on. Our main campaign in the party was to get the Labour Government to lift its ban on the May Day March, and in the process show them up as undemocratic. Using the Trades Councils as a front we determined to march whether Morrison wanted us to or not. We formed little action groups that, disguised as Trades Council members, would suddenly erupt into little battle teams determined to reach Trafalgar Square on the appointed day. I reached the Square all right, but it was in the back of a police van. Much to my surprise I found myself sentenced to two months' imprisonment. First, though, I had to do two weeks on remand, which didn't please me greatly. Not yet convicted I was worse off than if I had been. I was in my cell twenty-three hours out of twenty-four.

On conviction I found the treatment much better and settled down nicely to some mailbag sewing. There the tedium was relieved by my monocled neighbour who was convinced he was a duck, and quacked three times at regular intervals to prove it.

Then I determined to put the governor on the spot. I decided to ask for a copy of the selected works of Marx and Engels. Sure that he would refuse my request I got ready to play the martyr. Soon I was sent for, and marched in to see the Major.

Looking up at me he said, 'Well, Behan, I have read this book as I am required to do under the regulations,' he paused, and then went on, 'I feel bound to tell you that I have never been so damn bored in all my life. I just couldn't make head or tail of it. You can have it with my blessing, and much good may it do you.'

So to my annoyance I was lumbered with this great fat book, which is now wandering sadly round Brixton prison library.

The day I came out of jail the Korean war broke out. I knew this because I was met at the prison gates by a white faced comrade. His first words were, 'The North Koreans have attacked the South, and the Chinese are threatening to go in.'

Much later I heard that the Chinese 'volunteers' had been poured in because Mao feared that the North Korean Government were about to do a deal with the Yanks, with Stalin's blessing.

As soon as I got back to the house I was collared by Jack. 'Oh, you're back. Good. I want you to come with me to do a public meeting on Korea. We must answer the lies of the capitalist press.'

'A public meeting,' I gasped weakly.

He looked at me sternly. 'Brian, this is a crisis. It is our duty to show the face of the party.'

At that precise moment I would sooner have shown my arse, or anything else for that matter, but a public meeting was not my idea of the best way to spend my first day of freedom. In any case, our message went unheard. Apart from the natural hatred that all street traders have for loudspeaker vans, most of the crowd felt that the advance of the North Koreans meant the beginning of World War Three. Even within the van we weren't safe from the wrath of the crowd. They started to pound and beat on the side and then on the roof. Frustrated because the van stood firm, they started to rock the van back and forth like a pram, trying to topple it over. All the time the secretary was babbling away, putting the party line that the South had attacked the North. In desperation, I leaned over and grabbed the mike out of his hands.

'For Christ's sake,' I shouted, 'let's get out of here before they kill the two of us.' The hostility of the capitalist I expected, enjoyed even, but against the anger of the toilers I had no defence or excuse.

Troubles never come singly, for shortly after this I was involved in a libel action. Two be-knighted trade union leaders (both now dead) declared that I had slandered them in an article I had written in a flurry of revolutionary fervour. There wasn't much doubt about their chances if they went to court. I took the offending article to a solicitor, who did work for the party. Wanting us to take the offensive, I said, 'I can't see a word of libel in it.'

Thin and precise, he tapped his fingers together and smiled dryly. 'A word, my dear chap? There are thirteen libels so far, and I have only read the first paragraph. You simply can't go around saying this sort of thing, you know.'

I only knew about the libel because writs had been served on the printer and publisher. I hadn't received mine for the simple reason that the process-server couldn't make out which of the dozens of tenants, passing in and out of the house, was me. Once we realised who he was, sitting outside the house in his car, we plagued the life out of him. Everyone pretended to be me. We even had the women put on caps and sidle up to him, saying, 'Would you be looking for me, sir, by any chance?'

One day Reilly came staggering up the path, and the unfortunate writ-man walked smartly up to him and said, 'Mr Behan?'

Reilly tried to focus his glazed eyes on the man, and dumbly waggled his head up and down, upon which the delighted man slapped the writ into the palm of his hand. As he turned to go he was clutched into a beery bear-hug. 'I know what you're up to. I've heard about you dirty gazebos. You nancy boys, passing dirty notes about your filthy practices. Did you fancy me, then?' He raised his huge fist, and the poor man nearly died of fright.

'God no,' he cried. 'I'm Irish like yourself.'

'You don't sound Irish to me.'

'Well, it's me dad. He's as Irish as you are. You'd love him, you really would.'

Reilly was unwilling to let his victim go, and shouted, 'I would love no man, you dirty thing, ya.' He stuffed the writ down the man's front and shoved him away.

Still, I was caught in the end. I was strolling into a strike meeting, deep in conversation, when this character walked up and said, 'Hello, Brian. Long time no see.' I stuck out my paw to shake hands with him and he slapped the piece of paper into it. The writ called upon me to appear in the High Court of Chancery. In the end we had to print a lengthy apology.

Shortly after this, Celia and I decided to get married. Her father said we could have the two attic rooms if we would do them up ourselves. We made them lovely, working away, the two of us, till dead of night. I remember turning to see her tired face, all smudged with dust, and her smile gone weak with weariness. I reached out and grabbed her, delighted with her and the rooms and life in general. We were married a month, when the party asked me to go on a delegation to China. I was to travel via Czechoslovakia, Poland, Russia, and then stay for two months in the land of the little red men.

CHAPTER EIGHTEEN

Down Among the Red Men

I SAT in the hotel room and wondered what sort of man the Political Secretary of the Chinese Army would be. It was cool in here. Outside in the main Peking street the sun beat down unmercifully. Men with ropes tied around their bodies were pulling loads that an ass would have jibbed at. Behind me, the waiter asked, 'Anything to drink?' I shook my head. Chinese lemonade was beginning to play havoc with my stomach. Then I saw it, a great long black car, rounded like a beetle's back. Two tommy-gunners sat in the belly, while a motor-bike escort brought up the rear.

The man who got out was small and wore only a plain denim suit. Later, up in the room, I was astonished to see he wore no socks. When he spoke he addressed his remarks through his interpreter, never taking his eyes off me. The interpreter was the usual student kind. They all seem alike. 'The General hopes that you are having a pleasant stay in China.' I nodded that I was. 'He would like to know why you are willing to stay on in China. Perhaps you are fond of some pretty Chinese girl?' The last bit seemed to be his own manufacture. To avoid giving a direct answer I said, 'No, I am married.'

Did I really want to stay on? If someone had asked me in England to go to work for the Chinese I would have gone like a shot. Who could resist serving the march of the revolution, particularly as we saw it. Now after travelling 8,000 miles through Prague, Russia and China I wasn't so sure. Certainly I liked the place and the people better than Russia. They seemed livelier. The bloom of fighting Chiang and the war lords had not blown off. The Russians seemed tired, grey, Victorian. Here the kids ran round, demonstrating against everything. The city itself was lovely, if you kept to the right parts. From the sky it was like a park-land dotted here and there with trees. Apparently, the old emperors had refused to allow anyone the right to build higher than their palace walls. This allowed the trees to grow and fan out above many of the streets of small cool houses. But still my total feeling was one of disappointment.

It was true that women's feet were unbound, and the people at least ate something, but the great equality imposed by war was vanishing. The China of the Long March was no more. All round me were signs of two Chinas. In one you ate old paptoa leaves, in the other you wined and dined till your guts ached. I had just that night before attended a reception, given in our honour by a Chinese Mandarin. A business man who had his peace with the Republic. One of our delegation told me, with bated breath, that he had counted twenty-one courses. Drink, of course, was unlimited.

Then we went to North China. There the peasants seemed more like Aborigines than Chinamen. Almost coal black with the sun, they were too poor even to employ a donkey to pull the water pump. They used their own bodies. Standing treat they gave us some of their food. I swear to God a pig wouldn't touch it. For myself, coming straight from the Broadway Mansions, Shanghai, it seemed revolting.

Of course, learned men deny there can ever be absolute equality. Apart from the fact that they seem to be the ones guzzling, why can't we even get within spitting distance of it. In Moscow I had seen the same contrast. The city centre decked out like Hyde Park. But one morning early, I took a crafty tube ride to the outskirts. Here were slums, the likes of which I hadn't seen since Dublin. Worse still, I found building trade workers toiling away under the threat of armed guards. I was told the guards were there to prevent sabotage, but it seemed also a magnificently handy way to discourage agitation.

In Shanghai I had lived in a small exclusive suite, my every need catered for. While out on the river people barely kept body and soul together. I started the day with fresh strawberries and cream. The whole parasitical structure of hotels and flunkeys had been kept intact from Chiang. Again in East China I met the Commander of the East Chinese Army. He had taken over, lock, stock and barrel, the headquarters of his Nationalist predecessor. He lived in the most sumptuous elegant style, treating us to a marathon dinner at which we laughingly learned the use of chopsticks. This wasn't just a passing phase, one that would vanish as time went on. On the contrary, in Prague and older Communist capitals, my first shock was the sight of three path-

etic-looking men trying to fiddle in my Hotel Alcron. Again, when my
wife and I went to Bulgaria the contrast was even more pronounced.
We stayed at the Hotel Europa, Sofia. A beautiful city—my heart
warmed to the people in it. Every night they strolled or promenaded
as they called it up and down the streets. It seemed as though the whole
population came out to chat with one another. A city backed by the
Rila Mountains, where we were sent to stay.

Our house in the mountains was the home of a former tobacco mil-
lionaire. True to form the party had preserved not only his furnishings,
but even the special cook he employed. We shared this handy little
lodge with the Bulgarian Minister of Mines. A squat, powerfully
built man, he told me he had been a building trade worker. Sucking his
fingers, he said, 'You want to know how we survived under fascism?
Well, you must know we went underground, many of us making our
way to Russia. I stayed here, and when the Red Army advanced, led
the party comrades in settling accounts with our local scum. I met our
local fascist leader when we had thrown him into jail. He was terrified
of me. Like a rabbit, he dodged this way and that. I beat him to death
with these two hands.' He threw his two hands upon the table. With
all my hatred of fascism he made me feel he was Red fascist himself.

From Rila, the party flew us to Stalin on the Black Sea. Here, to
our relief, we seemed to be living in a more modest abode. Our 'guide'
from the Ministry of the Interior hastened to reassure us.

'No, comrades,' he said. 'This is only a temporary stopping place.
Soon we will go further up the coast.'

And we did. To the King of Bulgaria's private beach. Here we met
with Communists from all the parties in Europe. Italian, French,
Polish, etc. I sat up all night drinking with the, then, Polish Minister
of Finance. I fear the poor chap later met a most untimely end.

To guard us from prying eyes, the party had stationed armed guards
each end of the beach. Here in our Beach House we ate ripe melons
and discussed socialism. All delegations come back heavily laden. These
gifts are supposed to come from the grateful toilers of the country concerned. In fact they are nothing more or less than a bribe. One of our
delegation in China came back from a shopping expedition with so
much that I feared the plane would never get off the field.

To sweeten our path and to avoid the obvious, we were given a wad of currency to do what we liked with. When I was going to China a security man at the airport questioned my being able to go so far and live so long on such a pittance. I had exactly three English pounds to do it on. I smilingly told him, 'I would live frugally.' Still, for want of anything better, I defended what I saw there, and wrote glowing reports of children's homes, and big dams. This, despite the fact that outside our big house in the Rila Mountains an old woman of sixty sat all day long breaking a mountain of stones. Stopping by her in the drizzle I couldn't help asking myself where was workers' power.

I never did stay in China. The General said all right, but the delegation objected. They thought that if the idea got abroad that the Chinese were using delegation trips as recruitment points then doubt might be cast on the validity of the 'workers' delegations. I am glad now I didn't stay. Imagine being there after Hungary. Imagine being trapped there, disillusioned. The English men I met there led artificial lives. Operating with the news agency they dressed up in Chinese uniforms, which only had the effect of either making the skinny ones look like something out of Belsen, or the fat ones look like the fat man in Laurel and Hardy. In any case, if I couldn't make a revolution of my own I certainly didn't want to be a hanger-on after one already made.

CHAPTER NINETEEN

Black List

BACK IN England I was elected to the National Executive Committee of the Communist Party. Elected, hah! Selected by the top, and blessed by the sheep down below, would be a better description. By now I was a 'rank and file' leader.

I had been a shop steward on some of the biggest contracts and was chairman of the rank and file building workers' movement. Building workers are quite tough men, not easily impressed, so it can be truthfully said I was quite a fighter to gain the love and respect I did. For example, the day I came out of jail, the men on the site handed me ten pounds they had collected voluntarily and threatened to walk out if I wasn't reinstated at once. Which I was.

For me the real struggle on jobs has never had anything to do with wages. To me the fight to prevent indiscriminate sackings seemed infinitely more important. The dignity of the individual is not worth a curse if he can be thrown out at the whim of some foreman. How can you feel great if you have to gaze down a filthy manhole, ten foot deep, while you try and use it as a toilet. What sort of stinking world is it that denies the manual worker the same rights as the clerical.

Class distinction is still rampant in Britain, but it's between the clerical and the manual. So I fought every case of injustice bitterly and with a savagery born of having felt the whip bite deeply into my own flesh. Before long I went to the top of the master-builders' blacklist. It read:

'To all Site Agents.

Re Brian Desmond Behan—aged about thirty, labourer. Under no circumstances must this man be given employment on any site under our control. Please bring this to the attention of all personnel who engage labour.

J. Bollins. (Personnel Manager).

131

When it was shown to me, I just laughed. Inwardly I was pleased that my work had not gone unnoticed.

'I don't know what you're laughing at,' said the man. 'I risked my job bringing that out of the office.'

It was true enough. He had whipped it out of the personnel manager's files, expecting me to create about it. 'Well, what do you want me to do,' I said, 'play a brass band? I'm not surprised at this. It's a wonder they haven't tried to assassinate me, never mind blacklist me.'

The firm I was working for was building a thousand flats overlooking Wimbledon Common. Contrary to Marxian doom rattling, they were for workers. At first the rear guard still living in the spacious Victorian mansions had protested but they had had to give way. It was a beautiful site. We used the old mansions for stores, and picked the last pears in the doomed orchards. Set well back from the main road it was like walking down a country lane to get to our site. It was hard to get the job organised. The firm were already paying eightpence an hour on top of the union rate, plus plenty of overtime. Still, slowly but surely, we got one member, then two, then a dozen. The general foreman to avoid trouble decided to sack me. Unfortunately for him we had already suborned the charge-hand labourer, and he tipped us off. So forearmed we were able to counter his sack threat with a strike one. However, our agent believed there are more ways of killing a cat. 'He may be back but it won't be for long,' he told our spy. 'Put him down the hole with the dummy for company, he'll be begging for his cards by Friday.'

If I hadn't been told this in advance I would have baled out. The hole was the foundations for one of these sky-scraper blocks of flats. To get a firm footing the draglines had gouged out a hole thirty feet deep, and about a hundred wide. My job, with the dummy's help, was to trim up the bottom. Apart from the bottom being a sea of mud, the sun beating down on the confined space made it seem as hot as an oven. Another thing, the soil at that depth is dead, no worms, nothing, only clay that hasn't seen the light of day for a trillion years. Now it was soon to be covered again, lost to sight for ever. At first I tried to ignore the dummy but that seemed inhuman, so I tried speaking to him. Either someone had poisoned his mind against me or else he was just naturally vicious with everyone; anyway, every time I smiled at him he screamed like an ape with its throat cut. Some canteen women came standing round the top of the hole, and he nearly went mad, jumping and shaking himself most obscenely. He was an Irish dummy, so maybe some old farmer had tried to work him to death.

I once saw a letter to the Farming Correspondent of the *Irish Press*. The writer complained that he had hired, out of the county home, a labourer who was deaf and half blind. 'I pay him ten shillings a week, and yet I am compelled to stamp an insurance card for him.' I couldn't help but feel for the old dummy. I turned to see what he was doing, and a pickaxe missed my skull by inches. I think people who are deaf and dumb suffer horrors, imagining others thinking and talking about them in a spiteful fashion.

Rightly or wrongly, I put a lot of his hostility down to the firm, so I decided to go after them full blast. My opportunity came at the Friday canteen meeting. We had put in for twenty per cent bonus payment, which the firm had turned down. Some of the men were for immediate strike action. I opposed this.

'Brothers, let's face facts. If we go on strike we won't last more than a week. We'll get no backing from the union. They'll say it's unofficial and tell us to get back to work. No, the best way to hit this firm, and hit it hard, is to have a mass "go slow."'

This mass 'go slow' I had first tried out on the Festival of Britain site at Waterloo. The general foreman there had become so enraged that he put me washing the paws of the red lion that now stands outside Waterloo Station. Leo originally stood right in the middle of our site, and the general told my navvy ganger to put me there so that, as he said, 'Whenever I want to see where trouble is, I'll know where to look.'

The masses on the Putney site were highly intrigued by the idea of a 'go slow' and agreed to give it a try. 'Right,' quoth I, 'from now on we remain at work, but we do as little as possible. Nothing moves except your body and then only for breathing.'

One of the top cats was named Barker. He kept up a very good front. Always immaculately dressed, and sporting a red flower in his button-hole. He had a dark, heavy face, and this, coupled with his sleek, oily hair, made him seem like a high-class brothel-keeper rather than a building trade worker. He had taken over from old Venner. Although Venner had sacked me, I was sorry to see him go. He was a carpenter who had come right from the bottom. Tall and lean, theré was something very clean about him compared to Barker, whose first move was to try a bit of bribery on me. Sending for me one day he said, 'Now look here, Behan old chap. There's no need for you and I to get at loggerheads. I want a happy job, and I am sure we can all pull together.'

'Well,' I lied, 'that's all the stewards want.' In fact, what we wanted was control over the site so that we could use the union machine to put over our particular brand of socialism. On the Festival of Britain site we had been selling a hundred and eighty *Daily Workers* a day. We had passed the most obscure political resolutions, and above all, we had defended every last action of Joe Stalin's. All really by winning the reputation for being the best when it came to standing up to the bosses in the interests of the workers. Actually, if the employers had started behaving decently and agreed to a higher bonus, etc, we'd have been most disappointed and would have set about inventing some grievances. Sad to say, politics never have any such problem. For my efforts on the Festival site I had received the knighthood of election to the Communist Party Executive. So I listened to Mr Barker's proposals with great disdain.

'There you are,' he was saying. 'I knew you would see it my way. Now what do you say to a little celebration, eh? The two of us can go up town and have a night out. I've arranged for us to meet two little girlies . . .'

The thought of him pawing at women, young or old, made me feel ill. It seemed terrible that money could buy a creature like that access to a young body. He was most surprised when I primly refused to go, and informed him that I was married. Really, I should have said happily married; so many people are chained together like two goats tearing and locking their horns, that the word has different meanings depending on how yours is working out. After this rebuff Barker hardened his attitude; picking and pecking at me at every opportunity. Unfortunately for the poor man, he began his captaincy in the teeth of a raging gale. He had never before experienced a mass 'go slow.' Neither, for that matter, had I, not on this scale.

At first he challenged our right to 'work to rule'—our official name for it. I pointed out to him that it was impossible for anyone to define

a good day's work, particularly as we were not working piece-rates.
The first to fire were the unloading gang. Made up from all the dregs
of the rest of the gangs in the field, it couldn't have started in a better
place.

The leader of the gang was Big Galway. A West of Ireland man,
he was huge, even by their standards. I swear he could have wrestled a
gorilla. Next was Googan, who by night was a chucker-out in a
scruffy old picture house. Another member of the gang was Little Tip,
a Tipperary man of about five foot nothing. He had gone union
mad. The shop steward's job had given him the authority lack of
inches denied him. He kept his big Northumberland ganger in a constant state of fear by saying, 'Treat the lads well, Jim. We've got the
union in here now, and they're going in to see about gangers who don't.
So you're liable to find yourself going down the road.'

The first load to come on the job was bricks. Normally they are
taken off five to ten at a time, and four men can easily clear a wagon of
three thousand bricks in half an hour. To my dismay, Big Galway,
taking things to extremes, reached in one paw and took off one little
brick. Even then he didn't place it directly on the stack. No. He handed
it politely to Googan, who passed it along the line till it reached Tip.
Tip, gazing lovingly at it, gently dusted its bottom before he reluctantly put it down. At first the lorry driver thought this was some sort
of joke, and he took it in good part, smiling as he walked away to get a
cup of tea. A half hour later, when he came back, precisely thirty
bricks were off. Sitting back in his cabin he pondered and pondered.
Then the full horror of the 'go slow' dawned on him. Paid as he was
by the number of loads, he was losing big money through this caper.
Jumping out of his wagon, he started to curse most foully. Galway,
raising an enormous warning hand, admonished him.

'Now, now, my good man, control yourself, and please cease using
that dirty language. I will have you know I am a devout Roman
Catholic. By the way, you are in the union I take it?'

'No, I am not,' retorted the driver. 'And if you lot are union men,
by Christ, I'm glad I'm not. In any case, what the hell has that got to
do with it?'

'Well,' rebuked Galway, 'you may count yourself very lucky that
we unload a non-union man at all.'

Exhausted, the driver slumped back behind the wheel.

Two days later a wagon-load of cement came in. I was in Barker's office when the one-eyed O'Leary came pounding in.

'Christ Jesus,' he roared, 'I can't stand looking at that unloading gang any more. If I do, I'll be hung for one of them lazy, mickey-taking bastards.'

Barker walked rapidly over to the cement shed. There, six men were getting round one bag of cement; one at each corner and two in the middle, they walked like funeral pall bearers into the shed. To complete the comedy, Googan had placed his hat in the middle of each bag. Fortified by these examples, all the rest of the site tried to outdo one another.

At the enquiry later, Barker's bonus clerk presented evidence that the bricklayers laid one point seven bricks per man per day, compared to a normal output of six to seven hundred.

Despite the crippling effects of the 'go slow,' the firm only hardened. Far from giving in they determined to fight it right out to the last. They started by sacking me, and then, when the men remained on a 'go slow' to get me back, they sacked every man on the site.

From their point of view they had to. It was either the sack or give over site control to us, with the firm simply doing whatever we told them. In any case, a lot of our effort was to pose as 'militants' even if we gained nothing else. This pose would give us the support of the workers in their unions.

So I found myself out of work, back on the dole. I determined, from the very start, that I wouldn't accept any rubbishy old job I was handed, but rather, would concentrate on getting rid of them as fast as I could.

CHAPTER TWENTY

How to Succeed in not Doing Work

THE MOMENT I saw the site my heart sank. It was a sewerage job, with pipes that you could drive a double-decker bus through lying all round. When I asked for the general they pointed down a very wet slimy-looking hole. When he did come up I could hardly see his head peeping out over his very big rubber thigh-boots. Silently I handed him my green card from the Labour Exchange. Turning it over, he shot me a few dodgy old glances, and 'em'd' and 'aw'd' a bit.

'All right then,' he finally concluded. 'You can start Monday morning. Be here 7.30 sharp.'

As I walked away my heart sank. Was it for this stinking sewer I was to throw up my precious freedom. Working it all out after stoppages I would be exactly ten shillings a week better off. I felt a knot of hatred burst in my belly as I thought of what Monday would bring. Instead of my usual lie in till nine, then a quick snack and off to the Labour to sign on, I was to be up all night simply to get ten shillings. I groaned as I pictured my poor, clean feet being forced into cold wet boots. I re-lived again the fearful stench that had struck at me while I was passing that hole. Besides, I knew if I started that job it would break up my happy home. Things couldn't have gone better since I was on the dole. Never had I been sweeter-tempered, or felt more good-natured towards my kids. Yesterday I had taken them to the paddling pool and watched as they shrieked and splashed in the sun. Outside the gate I stopped and pondered the more. I made up my mind.

Wheeling round, I marched straight back to him. He was a short, broad man, a Welshmen, with a moustache. Welshmen seem to like a bit of hair round the upper lip. 'Well?' he said. 'Haven't I told you to start Monday? What more do you want?'

As I listened to his nasty voice I more than ever determined to be rid of him and his sewer.

'Well, governor, it's like this. I'd like to start on Monday, but I'm afraid it's out of the question.'

'Why is it?'

'I can't start because I have to go to the National Assistance Board to ask them for a grant to buy a pair of boots.'

'Boots—what in the 'ell are you talking about, boy?'

That did it, like the black man I hate being called 'boy.'

'Boots,' I cried. 'You're not deaf, are you? I said BOOTS. You surely don't expect me to go down that hole in these things.'

He looked down at my poor little black bits of leather, and agreed. 'No. I don't. I wouldn't expect any man to work in tiny little shoes like that. But surely, if you are a building trade worker, won't you have had some boots?'

'Oh yes,' I concurred. 'I did have some boots, heavy nailed ones, too, but the trouble is they were lying out in our backyard so long that they fell apart.'

He paled visibly. 'Well, for God's sake, how long were they out there?'

I pretended to think. 'Let me see now, why they must have been out there maybe three, no, four years. No, they were in our coal-hole a couple of years before then, on and off. I should say more like six years than four.'

The tip of his tongue was now feverishly wetting the corners of his moustache. 'Six years? Good heavens, man. Do you mean to stand there and tell me that you haven't worked in six years?'

I hastened to reassure him. 'Oh no. I have been working, but not in the building game.'

'Where then?' he asked.

Slowly and hesitantly I replied, 'Well, I was doing part-time work washing up in cafés and that.' Horror-struck, he tried to seize my green card back. Dodging him, I stood back and said, 'But governor. I can do this job, it doesn't matter about my back.'

'Back? Here, give me back that introduction card.'

'Oh no,' I cried. 'Surely you must at least need someone to make the tea?'

Springing up at me, he grabbed the card and said, 'You can forget about Monday morning. This job's full up.' Hurriedly he scrawled across the bottom of the card, 'Vacancies filled'. As we parted I asked him brightly, 'Should I give you a call next Monday, just in case?'

'Look son,' he said, 'you can give me a look in when your navvy boots come back from the dead.'

Back in base the same old crowd filled the seats, ninety per cent black, who genuinely wanted work, and wouldn't be offered it, and ten per cent poor white, who didn't want work at any price and would. Their disguises as non-workers would baffle, and have baffled, expert dodger-catchers. The champion shirker was a great bullock of an Irishman who denied his obvious physical well-being by saying his nerves were shattered. Once they said the country air would do him good, so they sent him to work with a landscape gardener. But after he sat down and commenced chewing the lawns like an ass, his career ended smartly. All attempts to frighten him were in vain. The head of our Assistance Board was a rather good-looking woman. Under her was a man they called the Dog. His method was to appear, roaring 'Behan! Behan!' in such a way as to terrify the timid. With the Bullock he failed miserably. All the Bullock did was to ignore him. The louder he shouted, 'Doran, Doran,' the less attention the Bullock paid him. Until finally, in desperation, he ran round the counter, and seizing the Bullock by the shoulder, shouted in his earhole, 'Isn't your name Doran?' The Bullock just turned his massive frame and catching him by the throat said, 'Mr Doran. That's my name.'

He then refused to answer any questions from the Dog on the grounds that he wasn't treating him with the proper respect due to a citizen. Then the female supervisor appeared.

With her black hair done up in a top-knot she was well preserved, a woman of about thirty-five. She had been sent from the Ministry of Works, and was still feeling her way. She decided to give the Bullock no quarter. Putting her hand on top of his file she said, 'Now, Mr Doran. You've been coming here for a quite long time, in fact, in the opinion of the Board, far too long.' If the size of his file was anything to go by then he must have started back in Old God's time. With a sheet for each visit, it now stood a foot off the counter, and needed quite an able man to carry it out.

'It's me nerves, Mrs.'

'Miss if you please, Mr Doran.' At the same time she glanced round and went on, 'There's no need to shout, Mr Doran.'

'I'm not shouting, Miss.' No, to him he wasn't. He conducted all his conversations as if you were three fields away.

He was a great lover of Russia, and predicted the opening of the gates of Paradise would commence with the further advance of the Red Army across Europe. Once when I was addressing a meeting on the inoffensive nature of the Warsaw Pact Powers he kept beating his points of encouragement out on the top of some poor man's car. As the dents got bigger my spiel trailed away. Behind him, the unfortunate car owner was trying to hold his massive arm in check. Frothing and spitting, he mistook the man for an interrupter. Throwing his two hands round the man's neck, he started to shake him and shout, 'You imperialist rat. By God, I will make an end to you.' Unfortunately he had got to know that I had been in Malin, a place he also had been.

'By God,' he would spit, 'I met one of them black-coated bastards again.' At this I felt bound to defend the Christian Brothers.

'Well,' I said, 'remember they had to take the leavings of the slums and idiot marriages, and try to rear them.' At this he would get frantic. 'You're as bad as them. By God, there will never be freedom in England or Ireland till the last bishop is strangled with the long gut of the last lord.'

Now he commenced scratching himself, much to the Supervisor's horror. Lifting up his shirt he began to trace his nails up and down his belly. Between watching his belly and trying to watch the file, the poor woman was nearly cross-eyed. Ignoring his scratching with difficulty she went on, 'Now, Mr Doran. You have been coming here some years now, and in the opinion of the Board, yours is a very serious case.'

Leaning forward he said, 'Oh, they're right mam, they are mam, I am a serious case. I am glad they're thinking about me. Now what I wanted today was a voucher for some winter clothes.'

Waving her hands, she replied, 'No, Mr Doran, you must rid yourself of this idea that all you have to do is come here with your hand out. Have you no pride?'

At this he commenced shouting again. 'You're like the rest. You think you can insult me just because of my afflictions. I have me pride, but sure, with all the money you're spending on war and the machinery of death you surely won't miss my little bit.'

At this she said patronisingly, 'Oh now, Mr Doran, all that's settled by Parliament, and that's quite outside our scope.' She sat back as though she had spoken of heaven.

'H'm,' went Doran. 'Parliament. I only wish to God I got my money as easy as them fellows. Sure that's the dearest Labour Exchange of the lot.'

By now he had half turned in the cubicle and was addressing the rest of the N.A.B. Her hands twitching, the Supervisor began to re--alise why the Dog had failed. 'Now,' she began, 'you must stop this nonsense and get yourself a job. I am afraid that until you make some effort the Board is reluctant to continue your running order.'

At this he began to rise up and down in his seat like a horseman. 'You would never do that,' he cried. 'You would never starve a white man.'

'I must point out, Mr Doran, that you are starving yourself. The Board is not compelled to hand out money to able-bodied idlers. And now I must conclude this interview.'

That was her mistake. Had she just got up and left, things might have worked out. But Doran, lunging forward, caught her by one hand while with the other he tore his shirt open. 'Look, look,' he cried. 'On this tormented flesh. Look at the effect my poor nerves have had on this body.'

Appalled, but fascinated, the woman watched him reach down to tear open his trousers. Leaping up, alarmed, she gasped, 'It's all right, Mr Doran, control yourself. Maybe the Board will reconsider. I will pay you this week and look at your case again.' Leaving the file, she beat a hasty retreat, leaving Doran smiling broadly to the packed audience.

The N.A.B. assigned a very vicious, evil-minded, red-headed man to my case. I was having a bath when he called. I shouted to my wife to tell him to wait, so that may not have created the best impression. And then he unfortunately sat down on a leaflet I was drafting, calling on the entire Labour Movement to unite in the struggle against unemployment. Rather grimly, he picked one up. 'I hope, Mr Behan, you're going to lead the masses by your good example in getting yourself a job. We wouldn't wish you to remain idle just so that others could get work.'

'Oh, I have high hopes of eventually finding a job.'

'Eventually, Mr Behan? I am afraid that's not quite good enough. If I may say so, you don't seem at all worried about your plight, but I can assure you that the Board is worried. Very worried indeed.'

'Well,' I laughed brightly, 'it's a good thing somebody's worried.'

At this he lifted his body and said sharply, 'This is no laughing matter, Mr Behan. I want you to make every effort to get yourself a job.' He turned to my wife. 'I know how you must feel, Mrs Behan.'

In fact he didn't. The four of us, my two little girls and us, had just spent two glorious weeks in the Isle of Sheppey. Glorious, not just because the weather was lovely, but also over our cavortings there lay no uneasy shadow of horrible work to go back to. We took with us a friend, also unemployed, but not perhaps as wise in the ways of exchange managers as he should have been. So that we would lose no money while on holiday, I made arrangements with him for us to sign on at the nearest Labour Exchange, in Sheppey. The only snag about this lark is that if there is no work in the exchange you're all right, if there is you're sunk. Our George nearly destroyed me in that exchange.

Marching in in front of me he said in a loud voice, 'We are down here on holiday, and we want to sign on.'

The manager nearly had a seizure. I ran as far from George as possible and denied all knowledge or association with him. Unfortunately, the manager had been alerted, and proceeded to cross-question me. A fat man with a bald head, he didn't look as if he would stand for any old buck. So I decided to play the daft Paddy act. To everything he said I turned big wondering eyes, and said, 'Is that so, sir . . . Is that a fact, sir.' Disarmed by my paddings, he said, 'I am glad you're not with that other scoundrel. I don't really know what the country is coming to when men go about like that.' Glancing around he said, 'I believe you're in luck. I have Mr Macey inside, he's looking for a scaffolder. Wait a minute, I will fetch him. Who knows, he might like the look of you and all your trouble will be over.'

Mr Macey looked more like a farmer than a builder. Apart from his pork-pie hat he also carried a heavy stick, a bad sign in any man. Humbly I extended my head towards him. 'Ah,' he said, 'so you're the chap the manager has been telling me about. Well, I want a good scaffolder. It's a good job, plenty of hours. Now have you any experience of scaffolding?'

'Scaffolding, sir. Is that what they hang men on?'

At first he thought I was joking, then when he saw my set, simple face, he heaved a heavy, heavy sigh. 'No, look here, if you're a building trade worker you will surely know what a scaffold is. You know, the framework outside the job the men stand on. . . . Oh, this is ridiculous. My God man, you know it's made up of ledgers and putlocks.'

At this I bounded forward. 'I am sorry, sir. I have never heard of a put lock. I've heard tell of a Yale lock or cupboard lock, but no Put Lock. Whereabouts do you put it?' I thought he was going to explode, but the manager intervened.

'I am so sorry, Mr Macey, to have troubled you. Please forgive me. These chaps are so stupid I wonder they ever find their way over here.'

Now back in my home the ginger man was telling me that my time on the N.A.B. was up. And he meant 'Up.' I had a feeling, after he was gone, that a man in a black uniform was due to cross my path, and he wouldn't be a bus driver. So I decided to take the very next job offered. Planking myself down I took up a position outside the vacancy box. As I did so, I suddenly got a blow on the back of the head that nearly knocked my eyes out. I swung round, half dazed, to see a big man walking away. I was making after him when the hatch-clerk called me. 'I saw that,' he said, like a man preparing to give evidence in the Old Bailey.

'You saw it, well, I felt it.'

'I know how you feel,' he cautioned, 'but remember that chap is not responsible for his actions. He is really a nut case. He lives alone with his mother, so you can see how it is.'

'No, I don't see how it is. Dozens of men live alone with their mother. They don't go round belting all in front of them. I am going after him, and when I've done with him he won't hit anyone else.' At this, most of the exchange gave a murmur of encouragement. Emboldened I raced out the door and found him standing there. 'Now look here,' I said. 'You have just hit me.'

There was something about his little watery eyes that confirmed what the hatch-clerk had said. He looked as mad as a March Hare. He had trouble in buttoning his coat across his chest, and it wasn't a barrier of fat. Looking at his hands I could well understand why my head had hurt. Glaring at me, he said, 'Yes, I did hit you, and I will hit you again.'

'But,' I protested, 'I have never seen you before in my life.'

'Oh yes you have, and I will teach you to keep your hands to yourself.'

I beat a hasty retreat, wondering which of the loony groups had put him on to me. But then, maybe it served me right for yielding and going to work.

The site I was sent to was presided over by an evil-looking man. Tall and thin, he seemed hungry for work. The site itself was tiny, no more than a couple of houses at the most. He seemed to resent my looking round.

'It's all right, Pat, there's room enough for you here. Be here to-morrow morning.' As I still kept looking round, he said, 'Seen everything, Pat, or have you missed something?'

Stung, I lashed out, 'Well, as a matter of fact I miss a lot of things. I see no canteen, no lavatory—or were you going to give us all a paper bag each, and then we could sling it over the wall. I see no drying room. What happens when it rains, you cut a drain down the back of our heads?'

Now his expression had changed to one of wariness. 'You don't half rabbit, Pat. I only hope you can work as much as you talk.'

Ignoring this, I kept on looking round. 'Still, I expect you know you are supposed to provide all these things. It's the law of the land, you know, that's what the Factory Acts are about. Besides, you can get done for indecency, if you don't provide a lavatory. Still, I expect we can get all that sorted out when I start.'

Even so, he stuck to his guns, and kept on saying, 'Start Monday then.' This mystified me. Supposing the N.A.B. had stage-managed the whole thing just waiting for me to refuse the job, and then they would pounce. I determined to be there first thing Monday morning.

But, alas. In the meantime one of my mates put the kibosh on the whole thing. Ringing up the bloke for a giggle, he said, 'Don't take any notes or look round, this is Brother Paul of the Third Order of Saint Francis speaking. I understand you are about to start the anti-Christ Behan on your job. Don't give succour to this devilish agitator.' On hearing a startled gasp at the other end, he banged the phone down.

On the Monday morning I toiled wearily to the site. As I rounded the corner of the road leading up to the site, I thought, Well, I am a quarter of an hour early, that's good. But there he was, barring my entrance up the road. Abject, he said, 'I am sorry, Pat, there's been a mistake. We are full up.' I looked at the site. 'But,' I said, 'there's nobody there. How the hell can you be full up?'

'Well,' he squirmed, 'we have to transfer men from other sites. Here, take this for your trouble.' He pressed a day's money into my hand, and left as rapidly as possible.

CHAPTER TWENTY-ONE

Russian Inventions

Now, after ten years in the Communist Party, we seemed no larger. All we did was hold our own. Our membership never went above thirty thousand, and this was only kept up by frantic recruiting drives in which, like the runner on the escalator, we kept running like mad just to stay in the same place. And yet in the union we were making great strides. I was now the London Delegate to our annual conference. Our positions on the Executive Committee were increasing. This, I used to think, was due to workers' love and respect of what we did on the jobs. In fact, it was partly that and partly because we had an election machine that our opponents lacked. Any similar gang of fanatics could have been equally successful.

Outside the unions, no one paid us the slightest attention. I stood as local Communist candidate and received precisely 181 votes. I felt bad about this until I noticed that nearly all our candidates received about the same. I have since concluded that this is the mathematical average of loonies in each area in Britain. I once said this to a Communist, and he said, 'No it's not. I got 190.'

People just didn't trust us. First there came the Russian brides; the refusal of the Russians to allow Russian wives of Englishmen to rejoin them in Britain. This seemed so heartless that even I couldn't justify it. Then came Tito's break with Stalin, and our whole word went topsy-turvey again. Tito became a running dog of the Imperialists, complete with blood dripping from inch-long fangs. To all who doubted we had the one line: 'You are believing the lies of Imperialism.' I came to blows with two of my best friends over the Korean war.

It seemed fantastic that our party was among the best fighters for workers' rights everywhere, except in Russia. 'Why haven't the workers in Russia got the right to strike?' No answer. 'Why aren't they free to leave their jobs as and when they please?' No answer.

'Is it true that the Communists are fiddling votes in the E.T.U.?'

This last was the hardest to bear. I, Simon Pure, had refused even to accept the increased delegation fees in my own union. The thought of Communists actually fiddling votes made me ill. I determined to fight, however hard it might be. I began to speak up on the Executive Committee. I found my first opportunity around the case of Dr Edith Bone.

'I value one hair on an old woman's head more than I do the whole Hungarian Government.'

Not a sound came from the rest of the Executive. Harry Pollitt had his hands clasped together, sitting up on a slightly raised platform.

'I want to know why we did nothing to save this woman from seven years imprisonment. If it is true that we knew nothing, then we stand exposed as idiots. Everyone else knew.'

John Gollan hastened to reasure the Executive. Small, thin, tubercular, he had a magically interesting voice. It was as though all his personality had run into his mouth. Resting one knee on his chair, he said, 'It's simply not true that we knew nothing. Some of us have been trying for years to get some satisfaction from the Hungarian Embassy. But we simply didn't get anywhere.'

It's no accident that the Scotch form the biggest part of the leadership of the British Communist Party. You only have to live in a place like Partick in Glasgow, to know why the residents provide more Communists per head of the population than anywhere else. Never have I seen anywhere such acres of grey granite blocks specially built to house the wage slaves. At least the slums we lived in in Dublin were hand-me-downs from the rich. So if we lived in squalor it was grand squalor. Our rooms were large and lofty. Our plastered ceilings works of art. Our door had an old duke's head for a knocker, while the one beside it had a rampant lion holding the knocker in his jaws. In Glasgow I saw my first 'Single end.' A little cubby hole scooped out of the wall, in which lived a man and four children. Right along the Clyde stretch mile after mile of these barrack blocks. It frightened me, because I had never really seen the effects of industrialisation before. The more prosperous English only supply the secondary leadership of the Communists. Pollitt was largely a historical accident. A large, fat, well-fed English tradesman, whose son went to Cambridge.

Now he signalled me to speak again. 'I want to know, then, who these comrades were who knew Dr Bone was in jail.' After a moment,

Gollan did a count. 'There was Dutt, Pollitt and myself.' He sat down as though to banish the idea. 'Then,' I went on, 'the position is even more disgraceful. To know that the woman was in jail, and do nothing about it.'

I was interrupted by Gollan. 'That again, comrades, is simply not true.' He had an earnest method of delivery which almost convinced you black was white. As he spoke he bent a long, thin hand out like a man stroking whiskers. 'We did everything we could to get Mrs Bone released. Comrade Pollitt and I made representations, time and again, to the Hungarian Embassy, without any success. Comrade Pollitt raised this and other cases in Moscow last year. You must remember that this was at the height of the cold war. We didn't want to give our enemies anything on a plate!'

'Even so,' I argued, 'that's no excuse. You should have informed this Executive, and run a public campaign in the *Daily Worker*. Look at how the workers would have respected us now if we had. How can anybody respect people who leave their own comrades to rot in jail, and say nothing about it.'

In front, someone scoffed. This angered me. 'I see nothing at all funny about the fate of a woman who has been a Communist all her life. Even if she wasn't, we should have done everything possible to get her out.' Still no reaction came from the rest. My tirade rolled on. 'We talk so much about the dignity of the individual and how we are out to elevate our working class. How can anyone take us seriously after this. They can hear a woman on the radio tell how she had spent seven years in solitary confinement in a so-called Communist country, for no reason whatever. Will they ever trust us when they know we did nothing to help her.'

This had no effect either. Not a single one of the thirty members of the Executive opened his mouth. And yet, individually, they were as pleasant a crowd as you could meet. Indeed, some of them held their posts as trade-union leaders on the basis of a bluff, hearty, hail-fellow-well-met attitude, that certainly had nothing on the surface, at least, to do with stony cold cells. Others were learned men, lecturers in their universities, some contributors to the leading cultural magazines. And yet here around the bones of one old lady they were dumb. In pursuit of an abstract political concept they were capable of defending the most monstrous barbarities. I knew, because I was one of them and had defended wickedness on the same basis. I had eliminated the individual from the centre of things, and substituted the machine. The aim, the goal, all else was secondary. Indeed, I had taken pride in my ability to subordinate things to the needs of the party. Now at least I was determined to do something. I pressed a resolution.

'I want this executive to publicly condemn the imprisonment of Dr Edith Bone.' The vote was thirty-two against my resolution, one for. Then I tried another tack.

'I want this executive to deplore the conduct of the three comrades in keeping this a secret from the rest of the executive.'

Again thirty-two votes to one.

That night I told my wife I intended resigning from the Executive.

'But why do they do it?' she said.

'Habit,' I mused, 'and a mixture of opportunist crankiness. Look at some of the trade unionists, born in the time of slumps; they see state control of everything as being the answer. In fact, it's not socialism at all, or if it is then the state-owned brothels in Italy are laying the foundations for socialism. The other part are demoralised, middle-class people, the same as those who flocked to Hitler. And the rest, cranks, mainly, look at my vote in the local elections.'

My wife laughed. My standing for the local council was one of our key jokes. I had secured the outstanding vote of 181, after ten weeks pounding doors, and speaking to empty school halls. My nearest Labour candidate got 2,000, and hardly walked out of the committee room.

'It's a Russian invention, the Communist Party. It has nothing to do really with the workers here, and they know it. Only a certain number of cranks in each area will vote for the Communists.'

My local branch was a case in point. Hot from one wordy congress, I called an emergency meeting of the branch to hear a report back. I had a total audience of four, which consisted of one man, scratching his girl friend's back, and one old lady, who, at the end of a two-hour tirade, woke up, shouting, 'They're sitting on my window sill again.' They were some hooligans who tormented her at home, so she came out to meetings.

'No,' I went on, 'the real socialists in Britain are the Socialist Party of Great Britain, or the Independent Labour Party. They are the two pieces of the old social democratic federation that really represented the state capitalists in Britain. The Communists simply represent Russian State capitalism.' Unfortunately, my wife was asleep, and so I was going on to our dog Randy.

The following day I found that I didn't need to resign from the Executive, I was going to get kicked off.

For some time now I had been running wild in my union, demanding all sorts of changes from the other party members, particularly those in full time positions. Basically I held that one of the problems in the unions was that the officials tended to live lives completely distinct from the members they were supposed to represent. I wanted a stronger movement of the rank and file, with the emphasis against corruption.

I was getting more and more disgusted with the way in which ordinary workers were being corrupted through visits to the Soviet and other Embassies. At first I wallowed in it, and thought it my due. Gradually, it assumed nightmare proportions. At one 'do' I went to, there was a great red carpet stretching right from the entrance to the kerb. At the top of it stood a real live Major Domo. Picking up my card I heard him intone, 'Mr and Mrs Behan.' But for the hammer and sickle, I would have mistaken it for the Dorchester. All the Hungry Tories of the Labour Party come to these 'do's'. Standing round the heavily laden tables, they wait for six-thirty like a greyhound at White City waits for the box to open. Then they are in to the kill. Those with long practice weave in and around the tables, stuffing their gobs as though they had never had a feed for days. At one of these functions I was amazed to see a leading Communist being carried out, drunk to the world. How can any so-called Communist justify this while workers in those countries lived on short rations for the cause? Once I saw the hired waiters stuffing their pockets with the loose fags. I said nothing. After all, maybe they were establishing workers' control. I followed their example and stuffed my own with what was left.

I told my wife I was attending no more 'do's.' The union money I had accepted quite gaily. For a week at conference it worked out at £27. This, while the basic wage was ten pounds, seemed to me, initially, a small reward for militant struggle. But then, if you had with that a week by the sea and various other junketings, it didn't seem as though we were really getting down to the members' business. Looking back I can see now that our so-called political links were really the stumbling block. Instead of recognising capitalism and fighting like capitalists for the biggest share, we pursued a mirage of Labour in power to solve our problems. We killed more Tories in our resolution than have ever lived or breathed, but could not negotiate a forty-four hour guaranteed week. Labour and Communist flogged themselves to death at the expense of the membership. No wonder the members ran out of the branches screaming 'All I ever hear in there is politics.'

My Executive said they disliked the way I went about things in the union, though not necessarily with my policy. 'So,' said Pollitt, 'we can't support your re-election to the Executive committee.' I made a little fight of it, and picked up one delegate vote in every three.

It was during this time that the boil that was Hungary burst. It spilled its pus of rape, looting and murder right across Europe. Like every Communist I was in a turmoil. The Stalin revelations had knocked me sideways; the Hungarian revolution turned me upside down. At first I tried to go along with the party line, even to the extent of echoing the rubbish that the strikers were paid agents. Then I swung over to the other view, and marched to an extended Executive meeting at the Holborn Hall, to submit a resolution that called for the withdrawal of Soviet troops, and the entry of United Nations' delegates to supervise free elections. Coming out of the meeting I was very nearly assaulted by an old Communist virago from Leeds, who wanted to know 'whose game I was playing.'

That night, Mindzenty came on the radio and I changed sides again. I was convinced I could now see the hand of the Papacy in the revolution. Even if it was, it was doing damn good work. To my shame I rescinded my resolution and put one the following day, calling for full support for Kadar and the Russian troops. It may have made little or no difference, but I would be a much happier person today if I had've fought harder for people who were resisting the guns and tanks of state capitalism. I suppose, while England holds people like O'Casey, who looked upon Hungary as 'a cruel necessity,' that the Communist will never be short of an apology. How terrible to be changed from an ordinary human being into a defender of criminal excesses under the guise of historical necessity.

Soon after this I decided to leave the Communist Party.

CHAPTER TWENTY-TWO

South Bank

IN 1959 I went to work on the South Bank for the second time. This time my old lion looked out, while the Shell building was stacked three-hundred feet up in the air.

Here, one of the biggest building disputes in history was to be fought out, a dispute that began with the sacking of two thousand men.

All round the edge of the crater the draglines lifted their iron necks and then sent their teeth darting down like a great buzzard's beaks. Remorselessly they tore at the ground like a pack of hungry hyaenas round the body of an elephant. Deeper and deeper grew the cavity until it began to look like the great arsehole of all creation. Then into it climbed the carpenters and steelfixers; on platforms ninety feet below ground they shored up the avenging clay with struts of timber and steel. Then from a swan-like crane, with its rider perched one hundred and fifty feet up, comes an endless golden, thick, creamy porridge that will set rock hard and carry the monster on its back. I only had eyes for organisation. Four thousand men, five years a-building. Link them to the Isle of Grain, the Atomic Power Station at Bradwell, and you had an army of 12,000. Imagine 12,000, enough to run a newspaper, buy a loud-speaker van or to cost over £100,000 a week if they all went slow together.

My mate was talking, 'By the way, I am the scaffolder's steward, and this is a ticket job.'

I just growled—part of my plan was to lie low and then emerge like a ravening lion. I would pretend hatred of all things union. 'Well,' he went on, 'we aren't too hard on new starters. We give them a couple of weeks, but if you aren't in by then, out you go.'

Now we had to go down the hole. Our task was to run a scaffold round the bottom for the chippies. Vast, like a canyon floor, there was still no room. In an area of twenty feet a crane was dropping sections of a concrete blow pipe. Behind us, welders were sticking a steel frame together before sinking it for all time. In front, the bucket of a digger was dropping thirty feet before it came up, raking and tearing out mouthfuls of clay and stones. Above us, in a ring round the edge, about thirty diggers all rocked back and forth, eating like giant pterodactyls. By half past four it was dark. But still the earth got no slumber. Bank after bank of searchlights lit up the hard frosty air; sparks from a welder's torch lit up his face, like a steel-helmeted Ku Klux Klan mask. A tremendous air of seething activity gripped the meanest tea boy. A big navvy, wearing a huge sombrero, is shouting MacAlpine's Fusiliers:

> Get out in the morning, stripped to the skin,
> And earn your bonus for Darky Fin.
> And then down the glen rode MacAlpine's men,
> With their fife and drum behind them.
> It was in the pub they drank their sub
> and it's in the spike you'll find them.
> They drank their sub, they drank their beer,
> they drank it with good cheer.
> And now we are on the road again.
> God damn and blast the beer.

'Hey, Ginger,' a man calls up to me, 'did you have it in last night.' I laughed, because in fact I had. Here on the South Bank of the Thames at Waterloo, Mac's men wrestled and fought with that great bear earth while sergeant death stretched his fingers round every throat. Four men died before that silly roof was stuck on, like a clown's hat on top of a grizzly bear's head. Then the hooters wailed and wailed. They screamed out against the death of a man crushed under the wheels of a wagon in the murky half-light. Work stops. What man can think of work looking in the face of death? Death is the only equaliser. A falling man will be smashed no matter how strong. The men stream off out the gates, leaving the jibs of cranes swinging silently pointing towards the moon. It's not the firm's fault, but they are blamed just the same. The men know that even if the firm are blameless it is always their own kind who lie crushed and mangled beneath the planner's beams.

The following day the man is gone and all but forgotten. A warm sun stretches the back, and makes it tingle with life. Bonus is on the agenda again. How much have we to come for last week? How much can we earn for next? Is it true the bonus clerk is on the fiddle? What a poxy lot of targets! How can you make anything when you have to pay for the services of the crane? Why doesn't the bloody union draw up targets and get the employer to agree to them before the bastard job starts? 'Too busy poncing about talking politics. What has politics got to do with the likes of you and me. It's a load of ballsology really.' 'I've a good mind not to pay the swine any more. All they do is make for coffee shops and drink tea.'

'Listen, have you heard the one about the queer teddy bear. No? Well, he threw his paw across the table.'

'Very funny. Give us up a few lengths of four by two. Here comes that ticket-steward again. I reckon he lives in that office, but we have to carry him. You know it all comes out of our bonus.'

'Listen, if there's any more trouble on this job I'm pulling out. Strike, strike, strike all the time. Look, we lose more time over meetings. We have a meeting nearly every day now. The firm won't stand for it you know.'

'No?'

'Not likely. Do you think they're going to have a load of Commies run this job. That's all they are, you know.'

'Who?'

'The stewards, of course, who do you think I mean, you dozey 'aporth?'

'I hear the firm is going to sack the lot.'

'I shouldn't wonder if it's true, they're bound to have a sort out. Things can't go on like this.'

In a big office overlooking Hyde Park another discussion is taking place.

'Are you sure there is nothing else we can do?'

'Nothing, old boy. I can assure you we have the union's O.K. on this, they know what we have to deal with.'

'I still wonder if we are doing the right thing. We never seem to tell the men anything. No wonder they believe the first loud mouth they hear.'

'Look here, old chap, that's hardly fair, after all, we pay union rates and conditions. But we are in the grip of trained agitators.'

'H'm, I wish it was all as simple as that. If we did our job, what could they find to agitate about. If only you had accepted my profit-sharing and consultation scheme.'

'Look here, my dear fellow, we can't go back over that again. We have been building for years without any trouble like this.'

'But all our men are casual, they have no status, we take them on one job and lose them when it's finished. No wonder they don't feel particularly loyal to us.'

I am at home when the telegram comes—'Come to site. All 2,000 being sacked Friday.' The sun was shining on the crowded meeting when I got there. A union official was telling the men there was nothing the union could do. 'We will watch the situation when the site re-opens, with a view to stopping victimisation.'

Another official feels that eventual public ownership of the industry is the only answer, though this same gentleman has, in my hearing, denounced British Railways, root and crop. Nationalisation-cum-State Capitalism—what a solution; our present employers are not big and bold enough. We must have the employer to end all employers.

At the stewards' meeting they debate what to do . . . I say, either fight or do nothing, what can we lose if we fight? We decide to fight. Alone now, no union backing, nothing. We turn savage. We determine to 'black Mac.' We are resolved that the site will not open without us. Feverishly now we prepare. First a conference of all building trade workers. Then a leaflet—fifty thousand of them putting our case, *Mac Produces Nothing*. Then a penny broadsheet with banner headings, photos, the lot. Our conference is held in the Holborn Hall, the attendance is varied. Dockers, bus drivers, builders, all listen to our case. Speaker after speaker praises our decision to stand and fight. I speak.

'If you really are with us in spirit, then be with us in the flesh next Monday morning, when Mac prepares to re-open.'

The delegates are silent. After all, it means the loss of a day's pay, the possibility of upsetting a not-so-bad governor. I press the point. 'Let us put a human wall round the site so that not a mouse will get through.'

On Monday I go to the site. Only a handful of men have turned up. My heart sinks, but I grab a poster and start walking up and down a very thin, skimpy line.

Then, just before eight o'clock, we hear the skirl of a bag-piper. From out of the mouth of Waterloo Station come the men of Abbey Wood Housing Site. Behind them the men from the building of the power station in Belvedere. Then over Waterloo Bridge come the lads from the *Daily Mirror* site. In five minutes we are the centre of a happy, excited throng, laughing and cat-calling to each other. Now our pickets are ten, twenty, thirty deep, and it's an honour to carry a poster. At eight o'clock the hooters blow, calling for work to begin. Not a single man goes in. A chorus of roars go up proclaiming that this day, at least, is ours.

It is the third week of the battle. Now the 'politicos' are appearing more openly, circling and mincing, trying to importune 'likely contacts.' One of them, so small that the sleeves of his raincoat hang down over his hands, rubs his hands over his sore eyes that make him look like a bull terrier, and mutters, 'There will be buckets of blood, yes, buckets of blood.' Yet he cringes when he passes John Law. He will live, like the Voyeur, through the actions of others.

It is early morning on the fourth week. Van after van pulls up under Waterloo Bridge. Out of them spill an endless stream of the lads in blue. Clattering down the embankment comes a patrol of mounted police. Their great haunched animals wheel and stamp in the road. Now comes a line of motor bikes, roaring round, making a complete circle. 'Paddy wagons' are now lining up, their attendants dropping their steps ready for their first customers. Swiftly the police spread out till they line every inch of the road. Our mass picket is pressed back, and slowly the gates yawn open to admit all those who have a mind to enter. Then we see what's afoot. A coach comes belting down the road. At first we see it's empty, and wonder why all the fuss about an empty coach. Then someone spots it. A cry goes up. 'The dirty, scabby bastards. They're lying down on the floor so we can't see them.'

Suddenly I feel afraid. What is there about us to terrify anyone. Surely we are the brotherhood of love? Imagine me in that coach. Shouldn't a man be free to do what he likes, work or not? Is our dictatorship any less evil than the employer's? But now the pickets start to shake and bend the line of police. The Inspector is screaming at the coach driver not to slow down, but to get to hell inside. Too late, the coach is stuck trying to angle its long body round the gate. Now the line of police is broken, and strikers' hands reach up to pull the driver out. Then a copper shouts over a walkie-talkie, 'Clear the gates.' Like cowboys at a rodeo the mounties ride in. Swiftly they isolate one group from another. Then they start picking out the leaders. Reaching down, they seize one man by the hair of the head and gallop off. Van after van is filled with struggling pickets. I sit in front of a broken-nosed bobby, who looks as though he's going to have me in a minute. I watch him very carefully. One thing I am sure of, the moment he comes at me I'm going to boot him good and proper. Another bobby comes in, his face split with the side edge of a picket poster. He doesn't exactly look as though he would 'suffer little children to come unto him.' Suddenly I realise what's wrong. There's not a single political fanatic in the coaches. They are waging the class war from the bottom of the Bridge café. If we peep through the slats we can see that violent struggles are still raging outside. But then suddenly everything falls silent. For the first time in five weeks we hear the triumphant roar of master dragline as he opens his mouth to begin devouring the earth as though nothing at all had happened.

CHAPTER TWENTY-THREE

Porridge

IN COURT I objected to my employers' solicitor conferring with the state prosecutor. The judge ignored me. Very rapidly I was sentenced to six weeks on both counts, though all I had done was address a public meeting. I pointed rather dramatically to MacAlpine's solicitor, and said, 'It's you who are sending me to jail.'

I had never been to a maximum security prison like Wandsworth, and it came as quite a shock. I had never seen a condemned cell before and it worried me a great deal that in a certain room in the same building they could take a man and choke him to death.

The sight of the condemned cell didn't worry me half as much as the look of the hangman's boss. We passed the cell every Monday morning on our way to the laundry. It looked just like any other cell. The only difference I could see was a heavy iron girder that jutted out.

The hangman's gobb had a face that you could chop concrete blocks on. A leathery face, he wore it like a mask, only on him it was the real thing. Generations of overlordship had gone to give the Brigadier that grim, 'life is no joke' exterior. It gave me the shivers to look at a man who would, without hesitation, proceed with you slowly to your place of strangulation. To see him you had to get your name down on Governor's call. Then you lined up with the other prisoners and waited for your name to be called. Standing beside him was the chief prison officer, and on his left the deputy. I just strolled in casually, and met a fearful roar from the Chief.

'Up on the mat, man. Shout your name and number.' The mat, a square just two by one, was there to ensure that if you bore the Governor any ill will you would never get near enough to vent it.

'Come on, man,' he glared, 'you do have a name?' Then he pulled out my file and started to read.

'Behan: "Three months for assault on a police officer."—H'm, this is your second time in prison for this offence, Behan. Do you have difficulty in controlling your animal instincts, then?'

I started to tell him that wasn't the case at all, but he shut me up saying, 'All right, all right. You can't make speeches in here. Now, what do you want to see me about?'

'Well,' I stammered, 'I didn't want to waste my time in here, and so I was hoping to get a course in English Literature.'

'English Literature.' He seemed impressed by that, but then he slammed my file down. 'Request denied. It would be a ridiculous waste of the taxpayers' money to let a man with such a short sentence begin a course of this sort.'

Prison libraries tend to include a large number of women's pot-boilers—*Through Peril to True Love*, etc. I snatched up one of these and spent the next ten minutes in my cell, cursing the 'hurry up' from the warder that had made me pick this load of rubbish. Its title was *Lady Barker's Jewels*.

One Sunday, in desperation and the thought of the long day and night alone in my cell, I decided to try and read it. From then on I laughed and laughed. A prisoner had gone through, line by line, and made the most amusing changes in this prissy, nonsensical work. In the story a policeman calls to investigate the robbery of jewels. The story opened:

'Inspector Bonallocak made it clear he was on the track of the thieves'—here, the prisoner had placed in brackets—(*he should know all Law are bleeding robbers*). Then where the young son and heir comes to greet his prospective mother-in-law he had written—*An Enry shoved his hand up her ladyships skirt and shouted three cheers for minge pie.*

Again at a scene where the family are reunited in happy harmony he substituted—*The father old sir Enry suggested they dance a ring a ring a rosy so they all made a daisy chain of their pricks and waltzed slowly round the great all.*

And so I found myself back on cleaning. My fellow cleaners were all short term like myself. Petty criminals, they ranged from house-breakers to handbag snatchers. Yet each in his own way was interesting. The handbag-snatcher was a very well spoken man who came of a good family. Somewhere in his assembly line a spare part had gone absent. The result was rather frightening. I would be walking round discussing Shaw and Joyce with him, when suddenly he would begin repeating, over and over again, his last sentence. It was for all the world like a record that gives out sweet music until suddenly it begins to go round and round in the same groove. Once started he kept repeating all the rest of the exercise time, right up the stairs and along his landing, till the heavy steel door clanged shut behind him.

One afternoon, as we were walking round, I said, mechanically, 'Isn't this a dreadful place.'

To my surprise he turned angrily on me and replied, 'Oh, I wouldn't say that.'

Annoyed at him disagreeing over something everyone else took for granted I said, sarcastically, 'You're not serious, surely?'

He had been walking a little in front of me. A medium-sized young man of thirty. He had an immense head and a very powerful neck. Now he turned on me in a fury and shouted, 'I like it here. I get three good meals a day, and a nice clean bed. And when I go out of here I shall do something big, like robbing a bank. I don't care if they catch me and send me back here for life. I get plenty of books in here, and plenty of time to read them.'

Then he just ignored me and marched off. Gradually we started to talk again and he told me his parents had more or less abandoned him when he became too big to control. Unable to work consistently he tramped from one end of England to the other. Tired of wandering, he felt jail was home.

Since he was in for snatching handbags, I asked him how he felt about knocking women about. This pleased him no end; he loved to talk about his 'work.'

'Oh, you've got me all wrong, old chap. I never knock them about, not worth it old boy. If they resist I nip off smartish. That's how I got in here. This funny old faggot got me by the arm, wouldn't let go, didn't want to strike a lady, got caught. Two hundred pounds in the bag. Lucky for her I didn't know that.'

In the cell next to him was the 'Indian Queer.' He was a dark-haired young man of about twenty. He had soft eyes, like squashed blackberries. He walked with his toes turned in and his hands shoved up his sleeves like a woman. Unlike the other queers he didn't use the red raddle off the walls to colour his lips. Neither did he burn the black facing page from his bible and use the charcoal to darken his eyebrows. The only reason he didn't was because he wasn't in, this time, for importuning, and he was afraid that if he was spotted as a queer he would lose his cushy job as a cleaner and be stuck on mailbags, or brush-making, where the screws could keep a closer eye on him. Jail seemed little or no hardship to him. He was surrounded by men who only had him to choose from. More than that, being a cleaner, he could dodge in and out of the cells with anyone that took his fancy. I asked him if they had ever tried to cure him.

'Oh yes,' he said. 'The last time I was in here it was for impor-tuning, then they tried everything—drugs, talks, and all that kind of thing. But I don't think they did me any good; only made me feel worse. I don't want them experimenting on me any more.'

We were standing beside the great back window that runs from the top landing to the bottom. The evening sun coming through made me feel warm and drowsy. Although Wandsworth is a maximum security prison, the cleaner screw left us alone. He would vanish for an hour at a time to God knows where. We were lucky to be cleaners up on the landings. We were out of the Chief's way. Not so the poor devils on centre cleaning. They had to clean the ring that was the meeting point of all the five wings, and the Chief's vantage point. He called in and out the wings, 'Open up the ones for exercise . . . Bang up the twos.' Being a cleaner there meant that you were literally under the Chief's feet all day.

'Look,' I asked, 'how did you become a queer?' Then I regretted poking my nosy nose into his affairs. He looked so sad and pensive. He replied, 'Oh, I think you would call it smother love. My mother loved us too much, you see; used to have us in her bed even when we were quite old.'

'But,' I said, 'your father, where was he?'

'I don't know,' he mused. 'In someone else's mother's bed, perhaps. Who knows.'

As he spoke he pursed his lips gently. 'Yes, my mother never wanted us to grow up. She used to dress us up like little girls. Then I was coming over on one of the P and O boats and I was caught by one of the stewards in a cabin; and that was that.'

6—WBE

When we were unobserved he used to do a mincing little provocative walk down the landing. One day I called after him, and when I said, 'By God, all you need is a skirt.'

'Oh my dear,' he laughed, 'I have one.'

'Do you dress as a woman?' I queried.

'Oh yes,' he said, 'and I bet you five pounds that if you saw me out in my skirt and bra you wouldn't know me.'

'A bra?' I laughed. 'But what do you fill it with?'

'Oh, oranges; what else? Big Jaffas of course.'

'Do you make a lot of money out of this racket?'

'Oh, about twenty or thirty pounds some weeks, some weeks none. It all depends on my clients. If they are free or not. One of them is a Labour M.P. and when his wife is away I stay with him for the weekend.'

'Well,' I tittered, 'at least you got the socialist message.'

He was a gentle, poor soul, unlike the other queers, who formed a laughing, brazen coven, and whom it was extremely dangerous to provoke or jeer. But after a while I began to get ashamed of having the queer for a partner as we walked round. Worse, he was beginning to bore me. Some queers are just queers, with them it's a full time job. So I began to dodge him at break times. At first he tried walking on his own. Even then he gave me little girlish waves as we passed that I had to steel myself to ignore. Gradually he got nearer and nearer to the pack, and then one day he joined them openly, giggling and screaming in high-pitched voices. Then I had to hunt round for a new mate to chat to.

Once on the No. 1 landing I had seen a sentence on a cell card that struck me like a punch in the mouth. It read: 'Sentence—Life Imprisonment.' Staggered by the finality of this I was curious to know who the unfortunate was. When he was pointed out to me I didn't know what to think. He walked with the old men and the cripples in the inner ring. He looked to be about sixty himself. I found no difficulty at all in striking up a conversation with him.

'You'll have read all about me, I expect?' I nodded, although I hadn't.

'I was the one who was condemned to death and then reprieved.'

'Oh, so you were in the death cell. What was it like?'

'Oh, much the same as any other you know. The only difference is, once you pass through that door you never come out again.'

'But they must take you out of it to hang you.'

'Well, not the one I was in. There you had a door in the middle of the wall opposite you, and when your time came they simply took you into the next room and that was that. Of course I knew they would never top me.'

'How could you be so sure?'

'Well,' he said, a bit annoyed, 'it was the evidence, don't you see. The police had to manufacture it all. I was framed, that was the long and short of it. My Counsel said he could never understand how they got a conviction.'

I felt a surge of anger go through me as I looked at this poor man, framed on a murder charge. So now I was really hearing what the police got up to.

'They're swine,' I said, 'dirty, filthy swine.'

'Who?' he asked.

'Why, the police of course. My God, it's one thing to frame a man for petty thieving, but to almost get you hung when you were innocent. This is monstrous.'

He looked at me very old-fashioned. 'Who said I was innocent?'

'But-t-t' I stuttered. 'You said the police framed you.'

'That's right, and they did, but I was guilty all right; and they knew it. They just had no evidence.'

At this I instinctively moved a pace away from him. So this was my first sight of a murderer. Now I began to see things in him I hadn't noticed before. His ears were flat back against his bony skull. His hands were veined and powerful.

'But who did you kill?'

At this his face grew grey and thoughtful. Up to now he had worn the air of a man of some importance not to be confused with a common tealeaf. A man of big events, high court dramas and Queen's Counsellors.

'It was all over my cat. I have had a lot of porridge in my time. A three stretch, here or there, then to cap it all, seven years for robbery with G.B.H.—short for Grievous Bodily Harm. Well, to continue, while I was on the moor I said to myself, "Now Frosty my lad, you're not getting any younger. These cold cells are murder on your old bones." So I made up my mind, no more bird for Frosty. I wasn't going to end my life in some cell.'

As he talked I looked round. Nothing seemed real and yet it was all too real. It was a cold, chill day, and above the hubbub of talk the great brick walls rose in solid masses. Around the edges of the yard someone had planted a few flowers but nothing could defeat the cindery track that dragged at our feet.

Behind us the blocks with fifteen-hundred peepholes rose up, topped by a huge pair of square chimneys. At each corner of the yard stood a screw; somewhat restive and slightly intimidated by his loneliness in the face of the mob of prisoners. I noticed that they always seemed to come to life again, just when our little bit of freedom was ending.

My murderer was saying: 'So I did my time and once I was outside I avoided the villains and got myself a nice little job. I was well set up in my own little room when it started. Someone was tormenting my poor little cat. At night when I came home she would be terrified. I couldn't bear this. You know what any animal is like to a lonely man. Well, I was determined to catch whoever was at it. So one day I cantered home a bit early. As I was coming up the stairs, Trixie, that's my cat, came up to me dragging her back leg behind her. It was my neighbour, and I had caught him redhanded. I went to see him but he came to the door with a length of hose pipe in his hand. I tried to argue with him, but he wasn't having any.'

At this point our exercise ended and we shuffled back to our cells. As I lay on my bed I wondered how I was going to endure this weekend. It was now 3 o'clock Saturday afternoon. Except for an hour's exercise tomorrow I was going to be in here till 9.30 Monday morning. I counted it up. Thirty-nine hours solitary confinement.

The following day I picked up with the lifer again, and nudged him to go on.

'Where was I? Ah, yes. I was telling you I wanted to see this joker that was tormenting my cat. I only wanted to tell him to leave my cat alone. But he wouldn't listen. He must have thought I was coming to ᴄort him out. He met me with a belt of that damned hose pipe. Well I need hardly tell you the rest. I really went for the bastard; what with my poor Trixie crying half the night I darted into my own gaff and picked up the first thing I could lay my hands on. It happened to be a chopper. Even then I had no intention of killing him. But seeing my hatchet he started to yell the place down. Well, you can imagine the state I was in. If he got to the police and told them I was chasing people with a hatchet I was finished. I was a cert for fourteen years P.D.'

I looked at him.

'Oh, you want to know what P.D. is. Well, it's Preventive Detention. Once you have had three times at the sessions the next time out they can dish you out as much porridge as they like, no matter what you've done. Look over there.'

He pointed to a big young man, shambling round.

'Well, he's due to go to Parkhurst to do a P.D. for eight years. All he did was knock off one-and-eightpence worth of grub from a caff in Leeds.'

'But that's fantastic.'

'Um, it may be but that's John Law. Well, I could see my little home, my job, the lot going for a Burton, so I ran after him and tried to get him to calm down.'

Now he seemed to get agitated as though he was still arguing with his victim.

'I kept saying, "Now look here, Jack, no one is going to hurt you," but he wouldn't pay me any heed. He was like a madman going on about getting to the police and belting me with that pipe. I tell you I lost my temper with him, so I banged him a couple of times with the flat of the hatchet. Then, I still don't know how, I found the blade was buried in his nut.'

He breathed heavily. Now the sun was shining and the circle of chattering prisoners looked for all the world like monks. The older men and the sick wore grey cloaks that made them look like something out of the Crimean war.

'Are you listening?' he growled.

'Oh,' I said. 'Well, I was just thinking the only really safe way to break out of here would be with a helicopter. Just fly it over the wall and away we go like birds.'

'Birds,' he scoffed, 'did you hear that daft Hymn we sang this morning in church, "Oh for the wings of a dove." Christ, if I had the wings of a dove that Chaplain wouldn't half get a shock seeing me get to hell out of here.'

We walked on and then looking at the ground he said, 'I won't end my days in here, you know.' I tried to look as though I believed this too.

'No, I have my appeal for a pardon going in. Well, what good can it do; keeping an old man like me locked up here till the day I die? All I want is to end my days outside.'

That night in my cell I tossed and turned, but couldn't sleep. I had now been in here for twenty-one hours, except for the one hour's exercise break. All my meals had been eaten here, and I still had another twelve hours to go. Playing on my mind was the story a con man had told me about my predecessor. The con man was a dirty animal, one of our cleaning squad, whom I suspected of stealing cobs of bread from the other men while they were in the brush and bag shops. I had more or less accused him of this and for spite he had told me what happened to the man who had had this cell before me.

One morning when they opened up he was standing in his corner facing the wall. Nothing the screws could do would make him turn round and face the other way. Eventually, of course, they got him by dint of three of them pulling and tugging. Well, two days later this man took his razor blade and ran it across both his eyeballs. Pieces of his eyes were found on the table when the screws went and found him sitting there with the blood streaming down his cheeks. The horror of this kept beating on my brain, and I felt it would keel right over soon. Even if it were a terrible lie he had made up to torment me the effect was the same. Even worse, was the knowledge that it had happened somewhere, and that it would happen again and again. Then I tried lying down, but as I lay on my side the wall, which was only a few inches away, seemed to press nearer and nearer until I felt it must devour me. I felt its presence was a malevolent thing, devoid of feeling or pity.

The wall had no softness, just course after course of lime-laid bricks that had beaten and killed generations of soft, slushy human beings. To escape, I walked to the window and tried to look out. The moment I stepped down again, I felt the feeling again. That wall; it seemed terrible that it should have the power to outlast me. It seemed a denial of all

humanity that you could be locked up here for life with the walls—
pitiless, hard, just watching you crumble and die. I longed to tear the
walls down, to let the sun beat into the dark corners of the cell. I
wanted to do what dozens of prisoners do every week, and have a small
smash-up. I wanted to beat every last brick into pulp, and burn every
door until it remained a mangled, twisted thing.

Men who smash up, start off by breaking the windows, the light
bulb, and any of the furniture they can manage. Then they start on
tearing up the blankets and sheets. By then the heavy squad has been
sent for. In Wandsworth they were the youngest and fittest screws.
They had their own special alarm, which sent them running for their
long, heavy canes. Armed with a mattress, they simply piled on top of
the destroyer, and shoved him into solitary without any bed or bedding.

Every prisoner leaving jail is interviewed by the Governor, or his
deputy, and asked if he has any complaints. Most men never have, because their minds are rapidly switching over to the outside. They want
to forget all about prison. I had to be different.

'Any complaints, Behan?'

'Yes, sir.'

So unexpected was my answer that the Chief rapidly dropped his
grin, and advanced towards me. Keeping one eye on his cane, I went
on: 'Well, sir, you did ask me if I had any.'

'All right, then, what is it; but don't give us a long political lecture,
for God's sake.'

'Well, sir, I think we are kept in our cells far too long. In fact, you
are breaking the law.'

At this he became very excited.

'What do you mean, we are breaking the law?'

'Well, sir. You know the sheet you give us to read when we come
in?'

He scoffed, 'Oh, a barrack room lawyer, eh? Well, go on, what did
your investigations reveal?'

Slightly nettled I said, 'They revealed this—that you are required
by law, that is, you and the prison commissioners' (I put that in to make
him see his place in the scheme of things), 'are bound to find us work

outside our cells for at least eight hours a day. Why, on cleaning, I wasn't doing four.'

At least he seemed to take it seriously.

'I know, Behan, what you say is true, but our hands are tied. There is nothing we would like more than to keep you chaps fully occupied. But it's out of our hands; if the taxpayer won't foot the bill. What on earth can we do?'

I was going to launch out into a long diatribe about priorities, and then I thought, 'What the hell. I am wasting my own time now. It's gone eight o'clock.' I turned to go, but with long practice he determined to have the parting shot.

'Good luck now, Behan, and don't let me see you get into trouble again.'

Determined not to be bested I stopped at the door: 'Look, I wasn't in any trouble before . . .' but before I could go on he almost screamed: 'For God's sake man, go!'

CHAPTER TWENTY-FOUR

Nationalisation

I CAME out of jail determined never to go in there again, unless I was absolutely sure of what I was fighting for. I determined, within the Trotskyist movement, to challenge anything that stank of sharp practice. If my movement couldn't be absolutely free; free of any taint of using its members, then I didn't want any part of it. So I went to a national council meeting, determined to do battle.

Outside the Communist Party at that time were fanatical little groups who waited to net the stranded fish for themselves. They were latter-day Communists hoping and praying for a return of a Trotskyite Russia. They rattled his poor old bones with all the fervour of black witch-doctors. Each little sect claimed that it was the inheritor of the revealed truth. Even the era of two European Popes had hardly seen such disputations. In fact, they possessed all the vices of the Communist Party and none of its virtues. In due course I was expelled for calling on the comrades to practise what they preached (one member told me he couldn't marry a girl because she wasn't a Jewess, and his mother would object). It happened at the National Council Meeting in the following manner.

'Comrades,' barked our General Secretary. 'We must see to it that every local Labour Party is won for our policy. The next Labour Government must extend nationalisation to all the key industries. We must take the control of these vital industries out of the hands of private enterprise. Anything less is a betrayal of the interests of the whole working class.' He was a small man, made revolutionary by his failure to make a fortune selling floor-polish door to door. Over his head was a banner 'Labour to Power.' He may have been little but he was saucy with it. Waving his glasses towards some university people, he warned, 'Some of our Comrades are too fond of the high life—they hold back from giving all to the movement. They must base themselves on the power of the class. I hope that when we come to the print-shop development fund the comrades will be able to report to us that they have managed to collect over our £300 target.' Twirling his mouth upwards he banged his two hands on the table and shouted, 'We are out to smash private enterprise. Is any sacrifice too great for that?' With that he sat down and the meeting shuffled its feet awkwardly. Then gulping down a drink of water he called for the first speaker in discussion. Hesitantly I raised my hand. 'I don't want to speak, but there is a little resolution I would like to put before this meeting.' Swiftly I walked up to the table and dropped my little typewritten note.

Putting on his glasses he picked it up and, holding it about a foot from his face, read it. First he turned white, then I thought he must surely burst out crying, he looked at me with such a tearful, reproachful face. Then he simply flung it on the ground and commenced polishing his glasses feverishly. Calmly I picked it up and started to read it out.

' "This meeting resolves to extend nationalisation and workers' control to the assets of our movement, namely the print-shop premises, etc." ' I might as well have exploded a hydrogen bomb. All shuffling ceased, and every eye turned on me as though I had three heads. I smiled good naturedly at our Secretary. 'Well, aren't the comrades even going to discuss this. What about all this workers' democracy we keep telling outsiders about?'

Growling, he glared at me. 'Discussion, discussion, I know the discussion you're going to have. None. Do you think we are going to allow you to slander those comrades who hold the property of this movement on trust for the rest of the movement? Oh no. We have had some experience of your type of disruption before. We can discuss our movement's policy, yes, but who owns what, never!' Then appearing to collect himself, he shouted, 'Alf, Bill, lock up those windows.' Turning to the rest of us he muttered grimly, 'I want all you comrades to appreciate that M.I.5 have now developed a new device which they simply point towards a window and pick up the sound vibrations that bounce off it.'

Beside me, a school teacher listened raptly, sucking his pipe all the while. Looking towards the wall our Secretary continued, 'I ask all comrades to speak with their backs to the window, and if possible direct your sound waves to the floor.'

At this point I turned round, convinced that no one could possibly be taking all this seriously. On the contrary, as one man, lecturers, trade unionists and working women turned their chairs away from the window and commenced looking to the ground. One man, a psycho-analyst in a big London hospital, was bent double, his waves smashing into the wood blocks. At this I began to feel nervous and to wish I was elsewhere. People who could believe this lunacy could well be capable of anything. But now two men were barring the door. As I made to go, my leader thrust himself in front of me.

'You're not going to insult this meeting by leaving now. You will have to stay here till you withdraw this filthy muck. It's an insult to the founders of our movement, men like Marx and Engels and our be-loved Leon Trotsky.'

'Oh for God's sake,' I retorted, 'you're like an old grave robber, rattling their poor old bones. Let them lie in peace. I want a simple answer to a simple question, are we prepared to nationalise our own property?'

At this he seemed to lose all control. He shot up into the air as if on fire. 'You must withdraw that. Old bones indeed. Comrades, I demand that Comrade Behan withdraws this insult to the whole Labour Move-ment.'

'Careful now,' I waggled a warning finger at him. 'You're talking towards the window. Remember the little men with their yokebuses pointed at you.' By now he was within inches of my face. He must have been eating garlic or something vile, because there was a terrible smell off his breath.

I drew my hand out, more to push him away than anything else. Thinking I was going to put one on him he leaped back, squealing like a frightened child. One of his henchmen ran at me and belted me across the noggin. Half dazed, I staggered to the floor. To my intense relief I saw the psycho-analyst coming to my aid. Taking off his left shoe he clouted me over the head, knocking me flat on my back; 'reactionary swine,' he muttered as he stood looking down at me.

CHAPTER TWENTY-FIVE

Something Rotten . . .

AFTER I was expelled by the Trotskyites I found it hard to get work. Then a good friend of mine, Jim Doyle, offered to take me on with him as a carpenter.

My first reaction to Jim's suggestion was one of fright.

'Me,' I said, 'start work with you as a joiner?'

'Yes,' he smiled, 'why not? The only one that can catch you out is me, and after all I am the foreman.'

The following day I presented my body to the site. I don't mind admitting I was nervous—very nervous. To chance my arm at some timber butchery out on a rough site was one thing. To present myself as a hardwood joiner about to transform an embassy was quite another.

Still, Doyle didn't seem worried. On the contrary, standing there with a puckish grin he welcomed me in. 'Now,' he grinned, 'you'll need an apron. Here, you better have this.' And whipping off his own he tied it round my waist. Sticking a hammer in my hand he led me into a vast ballroom, and introduced me to my mate. He was a long gloomy-looking Geordie, who was forever sniffling like a drug addict. From the start I could see he didn't go a lot on me. Still, I thought, it's either this or a hungry Christmas. Geordie and I had to put down a hardwood floor. After two minutes it was only Geordie. I couldn't get the nails to go in. No matter what I did the nails bent. I hit straight, I hit them sideways, suddenly I jumped them, tenderly I crept up on them and stroked them like a father; but not a damn nail could I get in. On my left Geordie was tearing away leaving me on a little island of my own.

To my horror the head sherang came bowling in with Jim. He was fat and red-faced. Smartly dressed, he sported a great red flower in his buttonhole that matched his fat whiskey nose. 'And these,' he smiled, 'are our new joiners, Doyle?' Jim standing with his ruler clasped behind his back rocked to and fro.

'Yes, sir, they are—and I must say, damn good men.'

'I'm pleased to hear it. I know how hard it is to get decent crafts-men these days.'

'Oh,' said Jim, 'you can depend on it these men know their stuff. I had a devil of a job finding them.'

I felt myself get redder and redder. Desperately I thought of making a dash for the lavatory. Too late. Standing right over me, Jim enthused, 'And this one, sir, is the best of the lot.'

You swine, I thought, hitting my poor thumb a terrible whack.

'Indeed,' exclaimed the general, 'I am very pleased to meet you, my man.' Through fear and embarrassment I turned and gave the man a good view of my rear. The poor man didn't know what to do for as fast as he tried to go round to see me I turned from him.

'Extraordinary,' he murmered, 'what a modest chap. Still, Doyle, I expect we had better leave them to get on with the good work.'

A few weeks went by and I was getting used to the job. It was a real Solomon—£21 a week and all in the warm and dry. And then I had to bump into Shanahan. Shanahan, a red-haired anarchist with a lean and hungry look, who had a way of looking at your possessions—especially your women—with the burning eyes of a ravening wolf. He was genuine in his ideals, for having absolutely nothing himself he couldn't help but gain from any share-out. Riddled, like most extreme poli-ticians, with sexual frustration, he had the unnerving habit of sitting himself opposite my girl and staring at her legs, for hours on end.

I first met him at the home of a rich publisher who was giving a lec-ture on primitive Communism. The flat was sumptuous and so too was the publisher's wife, who reclined on a low divan listening raptly to her husband's tirade. 'All property is theft,' he cried. 'We must break down the false barriers that modern society has built between us.'

'You're right, you're right,' cried Shanahan. Whereupon he leapt on to the divan and grabbing the startled wife crushed her hungrily to his bosom.

This was one of the shortest meetings I have ever attended. Any-way, feeling it was my duty I got him a job. True to form, no sooner was he in that than he got weaving. First he demanded a meeting of all the joiners. Pulling a fast one, he made me the shop steward. Then he suggested a weekly site meeting at which the toiling masses could air their cribs and get Joe Soap to go into the office with them.

Of course word got round town about this, and within a week every militant in the city was heading for our site. Soon the canteen meetings were like debates in the Houses of Parliament. Except that we had the lot. Tories, Labourites, Communists, Trotskyists, an Oherlite and a former Zen Buddhist (Surbiton branch). We discussed everything under the sun, except work. With each faction endeavouring to outdo the others, the demands rolled in thick and fast. For some weeks I had had complaints from the men about a strange smell. This smell struck them hardest when they were in the lift with a thin, weedy-looking character named Ernie. As none of them had the guts to challenge the man I just ignored them. Smelly, as he was called, found that when he got into the lift he had it all to himself. I was hanging a door when suddenly I got a whiff that would shave a bald horse. The stench was so powerful that I had to throw open the window and lean out. Between gulps of fresh air I asked him what he wanted.

'This is a union job, isn't it?'

I nodded assent.

'I thought there were to be no sackings without you shop stewards being informed?'

I nodded again.

'Well, I have just been paid off.'

'Without a reason?' I asked. He just looked dumbly at me.

At the mass meeting everyone seemed reluctant to speak. In their hearts the majority wished old Smelly anywhere but here. As I called for speakers there was the usual shuffle of feet and lowering of heads. Then it came, an election speech from a Communist who saw himself as the next divisional organiser of the union.

First he demanded to know why the shop stewards had not been consulted. Then he proposed that the sacking be postponed until we had discussed it with the general. Not to be outdone Shanahan reasoned that a man was paid for his work and not his smell. The Labourite felt that the Communist was piling up too many potential voters for the next union elections. He demanded that not only should Smelly be reinstated but also he should be given a full apology. The masses, bewildered by this torrent of resolutions, amendments and addendums, began to feel restive. Perhaps Smelly hadn't been so bad after all. At the last Shanahan demanded that the apology be delivered to the whole canteen in person, by the general foreman. He based his demand on the theory that as Smelly was a union man he represented the body of the broad labour movement and any insult to him was an insult to all.

The meeting with the management was awful. Poor Smelly stood in one corner while the general looked in another for imaginary papers. After some humming and hawing he told us that there had been a complaint from one of the embassy staff about the dreadful smell in the lifts. While he was reluctant to sack any man, Smelly had to go. I was on the point of brightly asking him how he could be sure it was Smelly that smelled when I almost choked with the fumes of the noxious breezes wafting forth from that brother. Still, I asked him to reply to this monstrous charge. The poor creature could only talk sideways and then with his eyes fixed on the ground.

'I don't smell,' he muttered. 'I used to, but I went to the Council and had my clothes done.'

Thrusting his hand out he placed before us a note from the Council cleansing department certifying that he had had a sulphur bath and that his clothes had been fumigated. His clothes were a simple boiler-suit that hung down off him like a scarecrow. Though not yet thirty he had the beaten look of a gypsy dog. At the same time any sympathy you felt was strangled by the sly furtive expression in his eyes.

Now the general did his father act. Throwing one arm round Smelly and facing in the opposite direction, he said: 'Look here, son, it's three weeks since you came in here with that bit of paper. Let's face it, old chap, you do have a strong body odour. Now I don't blame you, I will try to help you all I can, but reinstatement is quite out of the question. Don't mind those fellows out there, they couldn't care less about you. As a matter of fact some of the loudest complaints have come from them.'

So that was that. No apology, no reinstatement; all we got was a threat to sack the lot if we didn't get back to work immediately. At the ensuing meeting various steps were discussed. Striking was rejected on the grounds that we would lose money. Then someone proposed a go-slow. At this Shanahan called out:

'Go-slow, don't be daft. If we go any slower we will come to a full stop. Who's going to notice whether we go slow or not when we just carry on normal working?'

There was a certain amount of truth in this. Being a time and material contract things were more than cushy. I was just hoping to close the meeting and bid our brother Smelly 'adieu' when that animal Shanahan jumped up again.

'Hold it, brothers, I've got it. Not a go-slow or a strike but a stay-in strike.'

At this all heads swung up. 'Yes,' he went on, 'all we have to do is to lock ourselves in on the three top floors and occupy the building.' At this the Communist gave a derisive titter.

'And what good will locking ourselves in do, may I ask?'

At this Shanahan gave a wicked grin. 'A lot of good, as a matter of fact. In the first place we won't be out in the cold; in the second we are not only locking ourselves in, we are also locking the governor out. While we are in here no work can go on, we can lock the scabs out as well.'

The masses seemed to go for this in a big way. One of them asked, 'But what about grub? There's none here.' Another shouted across, 'Trust you, Taff, always thinking of your gut.' Someone else shouted, 'Never mind about the food—what about the drink?'

Shanahan, now in full command, called back, 'I have plans for all that, but I won't reveal them till the time comes.'

The most awful thing was that everybody—including the sober conservative plasterers—seemed to take for granted that we were going through with this lunacy. No one demanded a vote and when I suggested one I was laughed to scorn. Sadly I made my way to the office. The general was having a nice dinner of liver and bacon.

'I am sorry to interrupt your dinner,' I said.

'Oh, that's all right, Pat,' he replied, fork poised before his mouth. Hesitantly I went on: 'I just thought I'd better let you know what the lads have decided.'

'Well?' he asked impatiently. 'Have they gone back to work yet?'

'No, I am afraid they haven't.'

He looked at me venomously, 'I've had my instructions from head office to sack the lot, and by God I will.'

I waited, and he looked again. 'Well, Pat, did you want to tell me something?'

'No,' I muttered, 'nothing.'

That night a long file of men assembled outside the pay office. Inside Timey was shuffling an immense heap of insurance cards. Standing outside the office was the general with two security men. The first in the queue was Shanahan. Instead of proceeding with his cards out the door, he turned and dashed up the stairs. Puzzled, the general watched man after man file up instead of out. Suddenly he heard the crash of heavy hammers and the sound of heavy timber baulks being dragged acroos the floor.

The two security men dashed up the stairs and threw themselves against the door. 'Too late, my friends,' cried Shanahan. 'We're in and staying in. Now,' he cried, ploughing his way through the crowd in the room. 'Now for the propaganda.' He stuck a loud-hailer through the window and let go such a roar that all the pigeons for miles rose in a cloud and a passing motorist lost control of his vehicle and ended up to his axles in the ornamental fishpond which graced this once quiet London Square.

From another window Brother Spencer, the Labourite, was busy chucking handfuls of leaflets on top of the passers-by. Within a few minutes hundreds of people had gathered to see this extraordinary sight. Bewildered and embarrassed, the general ran up and down the pavement appealing to the people to pay no attention to Shanahan's lies. But he had no chance against the loud-hailer.

Shanahan called upon toilers below to show their support by bringing donations of food and drink to succour their embattled brothers. This put the poor old general in an awful bad way. His fine fat cheeks were droopy and shaking like a boxer dog's Almost weeping, he screamed up at Shanahan:

'You swine, you filthy, underhand swine. Why don't you come out on strike like men?'

His appeals fell on deaf ears. The large rectangular inspector patiently explained that legally the embassy was foreign territory and there was nothing he could do. At this final blow the general staggered away whimpering like a dog.

The following day the square was like a fairground. Job after job marched up with their banners and listened to rousing speeches from various speakers. By now, all talk of Smelly had vanished. Instead loud resolutions were passed denouncing the Tory Government, demanding freedom for the Lanky Sam Party of Ceylon and the lifting of import restrictions on Chinese pigs' bristles. Dramatically, Shanahan announced the first ceremonial hauling up of food, which had been donated by the women's section of the Aid for Class War Prisoners League.

To thunderous applause the first basket went aloft. Suddenly from the window came showers of crusts and loud shouts of 'Send us up some drink.' Laughing, some of the crowd went away and came back with a crate of brown ale spotted here and there with miniature whiskeys. Now some typists joined the throng from an office block across the way. McCluskey, who looked like a carthorse standing up straight on his hind legs, bellowed down: 'Send us up some women, will you there?'

Tittering and giggling one of the girls put one leg in the basket. McCluskey gave a sudden jerk and upended her. Enchanted by the sweet sight of two lovely thighs the basket literally flew up. In she went through the window screaming very delightfully. In seconds she was followed by her mates and the wild strains of 'There'll be a hot time in the old town tonight' floated down to the assembled toilers.

I was glad when it ended. I felt, too, that maybe Shanahan had been right. Smelly was a human being and deserved to get a living along with the rest of us. Alas, no sooner was one door opened than another was shut. The general announced a sort-out amongst the navvies, only this time he expressly avoided sacking Smelly. Again Shanahan did a war-dance and again we wearily took another decision to stop work. When the whistle went to get back after dinner we all stopped where we were, all except Smelly. Away he went on a steady old plod up the stairs. Outraged, I spurted after him.

'Surely,' I cried, 'you of all people are not going back to graft?' Dully he looked hard at the concrete step.

'Nothing to do with me,' he mumbled.

'Nothing to do with you? That's nice. Isn't it? Have you no regard for the union?'

'Union?' his lips twisted in what I suspect was his secret grin. 'Union? I'm not in any union.'

CHAPTER TWENTY-SIX

The Closed Shop

MY CAREER as a chippie nearly ended when the union determined to throw me out.

I was summoned to a branch meeting and told a motion for my expulsion was down for discussion. I spoke, but to no avail. I began: 'All my family are life long trade unionists. My father is the president of his union. I have not scabbed or stolen union money. Why expel me?'

I might as well have been addressing a council of the dead. My worthy brothers, members of the Amalgamated Society of Woodworkers, were bent on my exclusion from their midst. The reasons were open and hidden. The hidden were contained in a long document that had been circulated among all the branch committee. This document listed all my hundred and one crimes. Of course, as with all such organisations, I was never allowed to get a peep into it, or to answer any of its charges. Indeed, I would never have known of its existence but for the fact that my vice-chairman, Ron, a good friend of mine, told me of it.

The more open reason was given by my general secretary, Smith, who had honoured us with his presence. Speaking in a broad Scotch accent he said, 'I greatly admire Brother Behan, and I am perfectly sure that he believes in the things he speaks about. However, he has been a member of another union, they have expelled him and they don't take kindly to us admitting him as a member while he is not in good standing with them.'

So the unions, like the employers, had their own black list. The extraordinary thing was that I was being expelled now, when I had parted company with all political organisations. Probably if I had been a member of some gang of political loonery they would never have dared take such liberties. Still I made a little fight of it.

Turning to the rest of the branch I asked, 'Can anyone here give a reason as to why they want to take my ticket away, and possibly my livelihood?' Getting no answer (the branch secretary didn't even leave off marking in subs), I started to shout at the man next to me, 'Can you tell me why you are doing this?'

He just looked at the ground like a stupid pig. Then I felt as any man must who opposes the dictatorship of unions. How many men had I frightened? How many had I got sacked because they wouldn't join a union? And really what good were they as members recruited in that way? Now I was beginning to see the door of the closed shop from the other side, banged fast in my face. My shop was a ticket one. No ticket, no job.

A large black paragraph appeared in the union journal telling members that I was out. My one-time foreman, also a branch member, had testified to the branch that I was a good worker, and an early riser. All this would be in vain once the tribe in my job got to know I was out. I resolved to bluff my way, whatever happened.

One day my shop steward produced the union magazine at the dinner break in the joiner's shop under Somerset House. In front of the rest he asked, 'Does this have anything to do with you, Pat.' Seizing the paper I started doing a song and dance act: 'I am fed up with being taken for this bastard Behan, simply because I happen to have the same name. If anyone else does this they will find themselves the wrong end of legal writ for damages.' My steward shied off hurriedly. Any threat of the law will frighten the life out of an Englishman.

Then my foreman came at me on the same lines. I was working in a post office out near Croydon, when Cousin Alf bowls up and inquires, 'That's a funny name you've got, Pat. Behan.' Laughing he said, 'You're no relation of that daft playwright fella are you, by any chance?'

'Oh, no,' I replied. 'God no. I have nothing to do with that crowd.'

'Just as well,' his face became more serious. 'One of them is not far from being an anarchist, you know. He tried to stop them building that Shell-Mex house.' Scratching his head he thought, 'What was his name now. Michael, was it?'

'That's it,' I hastily interposed. 'Michael, that's his name. Sure, he's well known.'

Slapping me on the shoulders my foreman went off. Luckily in his mind this man Behan would have been huge, a demonic figure, with hypnotic powers capable of fooling men by the thousand. He never in his wildest dreams equated my poor form with this sort of man. Luckily for me.

In many ways unions are a foretaste of the undemocratic state, that total state capitalism or nationalisation would bring. There is no right to strike or not, as you please, within a union. In the majority of unions they laugh to scorn the idea of a secret ballot before strike action. And yet in what other way can workers really make up their minds whether or not an issue is serious enough to jeopardise the future of their families. Secret ballot would also ensure that the employer would be left under no illusion that it was only a few shop stewards bluffing, and that the lads would go back in a few days.

The closed shop is an evil tyranny whether exercised by doctors, dentists or butchers. For almost three years I have lived the life of a hunted man, fearful of someone realising who I was, and then the subsequent dismissal. Nevertheless, I shall never again rejoin any union, no matter what the cost to myself. Unions arose out of a scarcity. Scarcity of work, scarcity of goods. Scarcity of pity, compassion. The sooner we have an era of plenty in which a union that denies another the right to work will be no longer necessary, the better.

By now I had been thrown off the Communist Party Executive. Expelled by the Trots. Expelled by the Labour Party. And had left the anarchists. Suddenly I found myself with miles of time. No more rushing out to speak here or there. No longer did I have to canvas on a Saturday or Sunday, trying to sell silly papers to people not so silly as to buy them. So I began to go out walking with my family. I walked everywhere. Box Hill. Leith Hill. Headley Heath. Once, though, I chanced upon Sevenoaks, and took on more than I bargained for.

CHAPTER TWENTY-SEVEN

For a Time, then, I Journeyed with the Anarchists

IT WAS about this time that I joined the anarchists. My first meeting was a disappointment. Over all our heads was a picture of the anarchist God-head, Durruti. They too had their Khrushchev. Then, seeing a nice printing machine lying idle, I pulled one of the comrades to one side and asked, 'Why don't we do a little forgery on the oul machine.' This to me had two advantages. First it gave me access to a little loose cash, secondly, by flooding the market with false currency, surely we would undermine our enemy, the state, in no time. Unfortunately my words fell upon stony, not to say flinty ground. The comrade looked at me in horror. 'But that might mean police action. Our little movement being disrupted. We can't get into criminal activity like that.' Then he went round whispering that I was out to ruin the movement. Shades of Guy Fawkes. All this lot would ever plant in the basement of Parliament House would be mushrooms.

Another disturbing thing. Most of the Spanish anarchists who had fled from Franco thirty years before were now little capitalists. They either had a café or owned tenements, in some cases, both. All they did in honour of dear dead departed anarchism was to march out on every May Day carrying the black flag of the anarchists.

They rarely attended our meetings, and I was quite surprised one night to see one of them sitting there. He had brought his daughter with him, a beautiful girl with big brown eyes and long raven hair. He was like El Sordo, the hero of the film 'For Whom the Bell Tolls.'

Our chairman asked us all: 'I wonder which of us can help comrade Salvo. You see, he has an old house nearby and he wants a sort of caretaker for it.'

My mate Shanahan laughed, 'Well, he's got more than I have, for a start. I haven't even got anywhere to lay my head tonight.' As he spoke he started eyeing Salvo's daughter again. That's the fourth time he's raped that poor girl mentally, I thought. Her father only spoke a little English but it seemed sufficient. What he wanted was someone, preferably with no money, that he could sign the house over to. This would only be a nominal transaction, the real ownership remaining with Salvo. The object of the exercise was to fox the council and save Salvo from going to jail for not keeping it in a fit state of repair. Shanahan seemed only too anxious to help.

'I'm your man,' he said. 'I haven't got two brass farthings to rub together, so they won't get much out of me.' Casting his eyes on Salvo's daughter, he continued, 'And certainly I can always help you with little odd jobs you might have round the place.'

What the poor girl thought of us I don't know. We must have made a macabre sight, sitting in a ramshackle room full of pamphlets and tracts thirty years old. We were the leavings of the great movement that rolled across the American Prairie organising lumberjacks, wheat men, and cotton pickers. Any resemblance between us and them was purely coincidental. All we had was the eerie, ghostly feeling you find in crypts or very old houses.

Salvo didn't take too kindly to Shanahan moving into this house, but what could he do. The council had to see the new owner in residence. The trouble was Shanahan stayed and stayed and stayed. He even invited his friends and they had a ball. Hearing of his new domain I resolved to go and see him. The house was obviously on its last legs. I expect Salvo was waiting for the council to include it in a new slum-clearing scheme, the edges of which were already nibbling at the corner of the street. The houses on either side were already bandaged up in tin sheets ready for the chopper. As I entered the hall I looked up at the bare bones of the leaded window over the hall door. Before me the stairs ran, covered with dust, up and up. But Shanahan seemed quite at home in his solitude. He was in great form. Lying on his bed he gave me a gap-toothed grin.

'So you have come to see my property have you?'

Feeling he was getting a bit above himself I rebuked him, 'It's hardly your property, is it?'

He raised a dirty, smelly foot and picking a toenail, retorted gently 'I would say it is my property. After all, old Salvo signed it all over to me.'

His bed obviously hadn't been made in days. All round the room wine bottles were scattering. Because the floor was tilted he had his bed wedged up so that he looked as though he was in a boat. Behind him on top of an old chest of drawers a stuffed bird kept watch on two children of long ago, who were eternally running to meet a spurred horseman.

Then from over my head came a voice. Someone singing in Gaelic. 'You're not alone, then?'

'Oh no,' he smiled gently. 'No. I have invited a few of my friends to share my free lodgings. Old Salvo doesn't like it, but then look at how we can fiddle the N.A.B. for the rent. You know he's threatening violence.' With the word 'violent' he seemed to get violent himself. Jerking his body up he cried, 'Let that crafty Spaniard try his tricks on me and he will find himself met with the wrath of the wild Dublin Mountaineer.' With that he started to skip and leap like a goat. I had to laugh. I couldn't help it. Even as I did he peeped down the stairs. Letting go a wild 'Halloo' he summoned his tribe to do battle with the advancing enemy. There on the foot of the stairs were three Spaniards, Salvo and two more, armed with crowbars. By the look on their faces they might have been repelling a battalion of Moors. Shanahan's aides were a motley crew. One, a Cork man, had just come back from Paris and declared he wasn't sure which sex he was, yet. To this end he wore the weirdest coat you ever saw. It was black and long with a swallow tail. In appearance this made him the image of Count Dracula. His third *aide de Combat* was Mow, an old Trotskyist who made his living from stealing books in Foyles. He had embarrassed me once because the poor old devil had asked me to lunch with him at Lyons' Salad Bowl in the Tottenham Court Road, where you can take as much as you can carry on a plate for three bob. I think they changed the rule after seeing Mow. First he started to build a wall of slabs of stuffing. More expertly than any bricklayer he raised it up and up till it stood six inches high off his plate. Then he commenced shovelling in all the rest in the crater. By the time he reached the cash desk he could hardly see out over it. I never felt so ashamed in all my life. Not the Mow. He just kept on golloping as though nothing had happened. Now he was sinking all his political differences, and joining Shanahan in a fight to defend home and hearth. At first all you could hear was the Spaniards jabbering away, and Shanahan roaring and swinging a hammer. For the row was purely a propaganda war which Shanahan won hands down.

Almost beside himself he exploded, 'Get back, you Spanish dogs, before you lie in gores of blood. Don't think you can frighten ex-I.R.A. men, who lived and died on the mountains of sweet Tyrone.'

All the while, Dracula was singing some old dirge and grasping a stout banister rail at the same time. Old Mow could only keep shouting, 'a Trotskyist never surrenders to landlords or bosses.' Faced with this nonsense the Spaniards didn't know where they were. Old Salvo tried appeasement. 'Now come, come, Paddy, you know you were entitled to let me have my house back.'

'Paddy, is it?' screamed Shanahan, 'there is no Paddy here. It's not your house, it's ours, and what we have we will hold.'

Old Dracula began to advance, swinging his handle and humming away. Shanahan hit the stairs a few loud raps with his flooring hammer and then demanded they be gone. The Spaniards, bewildered by such witchery, beat a hasty retreat, mumbling and grumbling to each other. Laughing and jeering, Shanahan went back to his bed.

That night I shared their free lodgings. Outside it was pouring rain. The wind kept swishing the rain up and down the street. Aside from a few rattles the old house seemed set to weather the storm. Then came a thunderous crack. Then another, then another. Petrified, we both lay where we were wondering what was wrong. Then we heard footsteps coming down the stairs. Gripping his hammer, Shanahan made ready to repel boarders. But it was only Dracula, white Dracula now, covered all over in lath and plaster. 'They are driving in the roof,' he announced. 'I think it's time to bail out.'

Shanahan pondered a moment and then quickly wrapped up his dirty singlet in a *News of the World.* 'You know,' he said, as we went through the hall door, 'the Spaniards are a violent race, a violent race.'

Other anarchist property seemed much more securely held by the English comrades. I listened to one of them address a meeting on the need for rank and file control over leaders. Before he began he fitted up a big fat banked tape recorder and switched it on. Flattered because I thought he was recording a historic meeting, I jumped into the discussion first off, the moment he finished. To my disgust the conceited wretch immediately switched it off, leaving only his voice on the tape.

CHAPTER TWENTY-EIGHT

A Very Civil Servant

FLUSHED with my success as a carpenter I determined to try my hand as a joiner. The firm I worked for had a contract to maintain the furnishing in Government buildings. One day my foreman asked me, 'How are you on high-class furniture repairs, Pat?'

There's not a chair in my kitchen that doesn't look like a gaptoothed old man's mouth. Despite this I bravely ventured, 'Oh, all right.'

'Got your cards, then?' Carefully he sniffed all round my ticket and then, like Napoleon before Waterloo, handed me a sealed envelope. 'Give this to the Ministry foreman in the Houses of Parliament.'

I gulped. My God, my wild mind had never envisaged anything so drastic. Still I might as well be a poor man as a poor boy.

On a bright Monday morning I found myself marching through the stone entrance and down to the joiners' shop.

'And this,' said the joiner-foreman, 'will be for your tools.'

I gulped. In front of me yawned a steel press, seven foot by three. All round it antique furniture, some of it three or four hundred years old, lay awaiting my pleasure. The joiners' shop was round by the Chancellor's Gate, under the arch, turn left, and there you are; Guy Fawkes' country, under the Houses of Parliament. All round me dedicated men in white aprons were busy cutting, whittling, carving. My tools at that time were a little more than I had at the embassy. Now I was the proud possessor of a Woolworth's claw hammer, bought for three half-crowns, a pair of broken pinchers, and a rusty nail file. These I carried in a brown, greasy hold-all that was ripped and torn from years of wear. The foreman led me to an old, old table that King Arthur must have had many a fine feed off.

'Now, Brian. I want you and your mate to clean this top off, trim your arris's and get the whole thing ready for the polishers. Now about this broken leg. I suggest a stub tenon, but I leave that to you. Right, then, that lot should keep you happy for a while.'

My mate was a young cockney. Hair combed straight in front, he looked like a junior edition of Marlon Brando. As soon as he opened his box I knew he was the real thing. He had about twenty trays neatly built into it, for all the world like a doctor's box. Each tray was lined out with tools that I never dreamed existed. Laughing at my interest, he tapped the top of this box and said, 'Fancy eh. Well, I knocked it out when I was doing cabinet making.'

Timidly I put my poor filthy old bag beside it. Next he produced an oil stone and three rapid movements broke down a big plane and started to sharpen the blade. As he wiped the edge off on the palm of his hand he said, 'What made you start on for the Ministry, then?'

'Oh, I am not a Ministry man. I am a contractor to the Ministry.'

'Doesn't matter so long as you're a joiner. One thing I can't stand is these chancers.'

I shook my head in approval, damning all chancers with him.

Warming to his theme he spoke for every craftsman, dead or yet to die. 'No, Brian. I can't stand them. We get them, you know, on this lark. Downright deceitful I call it. We have to serve seven years of our life and along comes some geezer who hadn't served a minute and he calls himself a joiner. I blame the union for taking them in and giving them tickets. They won't get in down our branch, I can tell you.'

By now he had produced a whacking great mallet and a pearl-handled chisel. Not waiting for my answer he gave the table a few taps. Seeing me just standing there he called,

'Come on then, mate. Let's be having ye. Here, give that wedge a tap up for me.' Diving into the bag as quickly as possible I whipped out my Woolworth's hammer. Even then I wouldn't have been so bad, but the foreman chose that very moment to walk out of his office and right up to where I was standing. Panic-stricken, I let fly at the wedge, beating it soundly round the ear-hole again and again. As the foreman went past the wedge went crack. He paused, looked sideways, and then thinking he must be hearing things, shook his head and moved on. My mate, all business in his clean white apron looked ill. 'Christ, don't tell me it's broken, mate.' I nodded miserably. Shaking his head he swallowed hard. 'All right then, leave it to me. Will you clean off the top of the table while I do this.' I nodded eagerly. Any job that simple was right up my street. Walking out I returned carrying a pail of warm water. 'Eh, Lenny,' I called, 'where's the scrubbing brushes?'

He looked at me perplexed. 'Scrubbing brushes? What scrubbing brushes? Whatever are you going on about?'

'I want a scrubbing brush to clean off the top of this table.'

Leaving down his hammer and chisel he looked at me very sharply. 'Are you trying to take the piss out of me, or what. Because if you are you're going to be sorry. I don't happen to be Joe Muggins.'

I put down the bucket wearily, 'I may as well tell you the truth.'

'I know,' he interrupted. 'You're a carpenter who has been on the building sites, and has never done this type of work before. For Christ's sake, mate, I have heard this load of old nanny a dozen times if I have heard it once. But never mind, it's just as well you told me. Now we can get on. Look mate, I don't mind helping anybody so long as they're straight with it. Look, don't worry about it. Just get out your smoothing plane and run it over that table top. Only watch you don't tear up the grain.'

I just stood at the other end of the table. Looking at me he chided, 'Come on then, let's see that old plane moving.'

I heaved a heavy sigh, 'I can't. I haven't got one.'

'Oh no.'

'Oh yes.' Then I let it spill. 'I might as well tell you the lot. I am not even your much despised cousin, the carpenter, and these are all the tools I have got.' I turned the bag upside down, spilling my pinchers, my nail file, and a heap of old dust onto the table. To my relief he grinned.

'Now I know this is some sort of joke.' He looked around to see if any of the other joiners were in on it.

'I wish it was.'

'Oh come on now, mate. Turn it up. No one, not even a brass-necked Paddy, could have the front to come into a joiners' shop, in the Houses of Parliament, knowing nothing and with no tools.'

Now that he knew the awful truth I didn't feel so bad. Indeed, I now found grim satisfaction in pressing the point home. 'Well, you are looking at one now, and, as the man said, it's my life in your hands. You can tell the coddy if you like, but I couldn't join my hands in prayer let alone be a joiner.'

At this he began to groan and moan like the ghost of Hamlet's father. 'You know, if this foreman finds out he's just liable to boot me out with you as an accomplice.' The thought hadn't occurred to me, but it sounded promising. Standing back, he looked at me again. 'Well, I must say, you have guts, there's no denying that. But how in hell are you going to fool this coddy here? He's a City and Guilds man from way back. Look, do yourself a favour. Slip out and buy yourself, or borrow, a plane. It's something you just got to have. Look, go out now, and I will tell old Smithy you are out in the bog.'

More to get away than anything else I nodded agreement. Pulling on my coat, I dashed out into Parliament Square. Here everything looked peaceful. Brown-coated Yanks strolled round, taking lengthy snaps of Big Ben and the warlike Queen Boadicea. Still, my main thought now was to get away and find a phone. Over in Westminster tube station I rang loud alarm bells. Only one of my friends could help, and she lived at Walthamstow. So I went straight away to Victoria and caught a 38 bus that rolled me through miles of London streets right out to Walthamstow.

The woman did have a plane. Unfortunately, like all rude mechanics, she thought all planes were the same. So did I until I saw the one she offered me. Although it was the biggest plane I had ever held, it measured exactly four inches. It was a miniature block plane, something you would give a kid to play with. Without any effort I could close my hand right over it, concealing it completely from human sight. Down-hearted, I made my way back. I tried to slip into the shop unnoticed, but the foreman was standing there by the table looking at his watch.

'Now then, my son, aren't you having rather a longer tea break than usual. We are waiting on this table you know. Don't leave it all to your mate. Play the game, old chap, there's a good lad.'

As quick as I could I whipped off my coat to show willing. With an encouraging wink from Lenny I began to use the little plane. At the far end of the table he started off with a jack plane, eighteen inches long. Using both his hands he was soon whipping great long streamers of wood into the air. He stopped to wipe the sweat from his brow, and then stared in amazement at me. I was strolling round the table, the little plane snugly held in the palm of my hand like a derringer pistol.

From between my fingers came a thin, wispy thread of wood, that I hurriedly plucked and cast on the floor. Leaning on his plane he asked, 'Whatever have you got there, for gawd's sake?'

Red as a beetroot I tried to pass it all off as a joke. 'It's an Irish plane. They don't let them grow any bigger there.' The atmosphere went distinctly chilly. Lenny just closed his mouth grimly and said, 'Well, I have just as much of this nonsense as I can stand. You had better find someone else to drive round the bend.' Pulling on his coat he walked out the door, right past the foreman. Mystified, the foreman said, 'What got into your mate, then? He has a face fit to kill on him.'

I made no answer, only turned my back and pretended to work. At first I thought I must follow him, then I thought what the hell. I will stick it out here until I am thrown out. I was just bending over the table, when I got a tap on the shoulder. It was Lenny. 'Move over then, mate. Someone's got to finish this bloody job.' We worked away in silence then he said, 'Sorry I blew my top just now, but anyone would have done the same now, wouldn't they. Look, let me stay on the top and you trim the arris's on the legs. Only be careful to keep them equal all the way round. Run your gauge over them every now and again.' Not knowing what the hell he was talking about I just kept tearing away. As I worked I found to my intense relief that the little plane moved along quite nicely, and it became quite pleasurable to feel it slice line after line down the wood. Emboldened, I got a mad desire to plane and plane. Feeling a bit cocky I started to chat to Lenny. 'What made you come in the Ministry, Len?'

'Oh, I am lazy, Brian.'

The completeness of the answer floored me. 'Lazy?'

'Yes. I am just lazy. I just don't wanna work if I can help it.'

Curious, I said, 'Well, what do you want to do then?'

'Oh, have birds, a booze up at the weekend, more birds.'

'But don't you worry about a home, kids and all that sort of thing?'

'Me? Not likely. I see too much of what marriage does to my mates. Why, they never go anywhere, do anything. Might as well be dead. The minute a bird starts to talk to me about settling down that's me, mate. I'm off.'

I laughed, 'But you're a bloody pagan, you don't care about anything. I suppose you'd have a married woman just the same?'

He pondered on this. 'Yes, too true I would. The trouble is I haven't had the chance yet. So you want to watch out, mate. I will be round your house the minute you've gone out.' He laughed and then said, 'Look at this job. Start at nine, do nothing till twelve, two hours dinner, knock off half past four. Where would you get anything to be at this? Dinner hour back in the War Office, where I have my shop, I close up from twelve to two and have a good kip. If I get a weekend in I make up to twenty-four quid. That's not bad, is it? Still, how about you. How did you wind up in here?'

'Well, it's a long story. I was out of a job and my mate, who is a carpenter, suggested that I try our firm. Well, I did, and they sent me here.'

'But how come they never rumbled you?'

'Well, I had this mate of mine to cover me at the start. Really he carried me for the first couple of weeks. Well, in a way it was comical. Every time our foreman came round I was the only one on the job. Not that I was doing anything, mind you, except breaking poor Botty's expanding bit. Well, one day, our coddy shoots round, and creeping up behind me calls me to one side. "I have been watching you," he says. Well, I nearly died. I thought, Oh Christ, if he's been watching me it's all up. I am out the gate Friday. But believe it or not, the stroke he comes out with then is that he's most impressed by my work, and asked me how would I be on high-class pieces of furniture repair-work up town. Well, Christ, I didn't know what to say. Well, to cut a long story short, he insisted on parting me from my mate, and here I am.'

Some of the story I hadn't told Lenny. Of how I had been expelled from one union and then when I joined another the brothers in my old union applied a black list, and demanded that my new one fire me out too. Which they promptly did. I had learned bitterly how a union, by taking away your ticket, could condemn you to starve. I swore then that never again would I hold a union card, and I never have. Neither would I ever again compel any man to join anything he didn't wish to. All power corrupts and absolute power in the union sense is breeding a particularly vile dictatorship, because it is the dictatorship of one working man by another. It means that the worker has to carry not one set of employers, but about three, by the time he allows for shop stewards, district committee men and all the paraphernalia that goes with it. In anger, thinking of the night I had been expelled, I started to rip and tear at the legs. Lenny grabbed my hand and roared, 'Mind what you're about or you will have no leg left.' With all the gabbing I had shaved one leg down till it looked like a fat pencil. Sinking down onto his knees, he sighed, 'Well, we can't odds it, mate All the legs will have to be reduced to the size of this wonky one, otherwise it's going to look odd. I am afraid, mate, you will have to stay back at dinner hour and see what you can do with them. Take your time. We have from twelve to two, so there's no mad rush.'

But I did rush as soon as the shop was empty. I started to plane and pare, going from leg to leg with the sweat pouring off me. But the more excited I became the more mistakes I made. Now all I had gained, at the end of an hour, was the top of my thumbnail sliced off to the quick, and the other three legs looking like a stork's. As I looked at it the table top, solid and weighty, began to swing crazily about on its spindly legs, like a ship with its rudder gone in a violent storm.

It only wanted the joiner foreman or indeed any of the joiners to see it and I was finished. Then I remembered an old saying of my father's, 'Doctors bury their mistakes.' Now I reasoned, if a doctor could bury his, why couldn't I do the same? The more I thought of it the better I liked it. The table became my hateful enemy, a living indictment of my idiocy. A wooden tablet of my crimes. Like a murderer I crept to the door and peeped out. There was nobody about; good. I reached up and took down a big rip saw. Leaping at the staggering, cringing thing, I cut and cut even though its knots shrieked out against the ripping of the shark-like teeth of the saw. It held firm, even when it was three-quarters way through, then it gave up the ghost and collapsed in two halves on the floor. Delighted to see it fall a pitiful wreck I now gave it the *coup de grâce*. Swinging a heavy hammer, I pounded its poor anaemic legs into long splintery shreds. Fearful now, that after all my efforts might be discovered, I rushed to the door to see what was coming down the passage. To my delight it was only a messenger. Smiling to him I dodged back to my prey. Again I went to the door. My luck was in. There wasn't a soul about. Dragging some pieces I raced round the long, lofty cellar sticking a piece here and then there. I was just sweeping up the shavings when the foreman walked in. 'No dinner then Pat? Oh, I see you have finished the table then? Did the polishers come and pick it up?'

'No. I took it over for them.'

'You did, Pat. Well, that's very good of you, but it's really not your job you know. We have the furniture porters here for humping that stuff about. Not that I mind, but it's the other joiners. They wouldn't like to think you were waiting on yourself, the lazy lot of sods.' Looking at my worried frown he clapped his hand on my back. 'Oh, don't take it to heart, Pat. It might never happen again. Look, I have a little job for you and your mate as soon as he comes back. I will put you on it.'

I left the Houses of Parliament the following day for the Ministry of Aviation. As I was leaving, the foreman said, 'Don't forget. If ever you want to come on the permanent staff just let me know.' From there I went to a Ministry building in High Holborn, where, for nigh on two years, I sheltered from the foul winds of the class war.

My disruptive past seemed forgotten, but then I was interviewed by the *Daily Express*. Someone must have been feeling extra alert that day; it suddenly dawned on them, after only two years, that I, Brian Behan alias Brian Behan, was lurking in their *sanctum sanctorum*, cunningly disguised in a white apron.

A high Ministry official reached for his red, white and blue phone. Barking like a sergeant-major, he roused my sleepy foreman nodding away in the weald of Kent. 'You employ this man Behan; well then, he must be out of our aviation building this very day, lock, stock and tools.'

Poor Bert, standing to attention beside the 'phone, he promised all traces of the wretch would be purged afore the sun went down.

Dreading another Profumo-cum-Guy Burgess débâcle the Minister made another call. Police were to stand by prepared to recapture the basement at all costs.

The next morning came the reckoning. I was told to go. When I went below to pack my tools, I was surprised to find a policeman standing there with me. Anxiously I enquired his business of him. 'You have no right to be here and I am here to escort you off the premises,' he replied.

To assist him, my foreman and the Ministry's stood at the ready.

Then as the packing went on, a plain clothes man joined the spectators. To my enquiry as to why he was there he gave a curt, 'Mind your own business.'

In full pomp and majesty I was escorted upstairs by the plain clothes man, two uniformed men, plus my accommodation officer and another. As I reached the main entrance, the security man on the door gave a signal to the plain clothes man on the stairs.

Outside stood a patrol wagon with four more men ready to receive the body of Behan.

Sadly lugging my tool box I made my way out the door.

My foreman racing up from Kent had driven to another Ministry building to pick up the rest of my tools. By bell, book and candle the last remains of the joiner Behan were erased. All that is except a pair of rubber boots which stand as a lone monument to my hours of glory.

As an old mate once told me, 'Look here, Brian, a great American statesman said "It's all a load of balls." '

I suppose he was right.

CHAPTER TWENTY-NINE

Back to Work

Now I am a bricklayer, that most noble of trades. Men, who by working together, stand close to God and dignity. Great men who have laid bricks to the sky. Bricks to house, to warm, to keep us alive in the blasty winter nights. Yet men who look out to no pension, no sick pay, nothing. Their only guarantee—two hours notice on a Friday. Praise the lord, they are a scarce breed nowadays, who can 'jack' in a job anytime they like.

My first job as bricklayer was in Whitechapel. That rotting arm of London pointing out to the sea. A mixture of seamen, dockers, Jewish clothing shops, and Indians who never seem to do anything much.

One half of the hut was collapsing. Stepping carefully to avoid the sagging timbers the men picked up their tools. It was half past seven on a sharp August morning. Another day had begun. By tea-time the two corners were up; like gladiators the men stabbed their trowels into the heavy compo, and marched patiently up and down, swiftly laying the bricks. As the compo was swept from the boards a shout went floating down to the hod carriers.

'Muck up. Let's have your muck or money.'

Angrily the labourers filled the tin v-shaped panniers and started away up the ladders. Just then the whistle cut short a bricklayer as he reached for another trowel-full. 'Tea up.' Thankfully the men break ranks and make as fast as they can, without running, to the tin shed. When God made them he matched them. The men were a mixture. The bricklayers as always, mainly cockneys. The labourers, liquorice all sorts. The tea boy was a Liverpool man who had first come down four years ago to bury his mother-in-law and never returned to the shadow of the Royal Liver. Charlie Fagg was talking. Charlie had served his time as a bricklayer in prison. A hard-looking broad little man, he had a knife scar that ran into his mouth.

'This job is crazy,' he looked round for approval. 'Do you know, Mick, them three chimney stacks have all got to come down.'

'It's a crying shame,' concurred the Scouse, waving his fork, 'what with people waiting for houses. Do you know, this job is fourteen weeks behind.'

Another bricklayer sat munching sandwiches and looking hard at the floor. 'It's the architect's fault,' he said finally, 'some of the designs here are just daft.'

All the men sighed approval. Once again the nameless swine who arrived on the site armed with slip-ons to keep out the mud and poky umbrellas were found to be wanting. Back at work a bricklayer waited until the clerk of works came up, looking ominously at a drawing. He sang, 'Oh put it up, oh take it down, that's all we do when you're around.'

Flushing, the clerk said defensively, 'Well, we have got to get it right, Bill.'

The men smiled derisively. They knew a job fourteen weeks behind, with slums rising all round, was a job with a black cloud fixed firmly on the scaffold.

At this rate how could the slums be pulled down? From the scaffold they could look straight into rooms through windows that lacked glass. Yet people peeped out from time to time, giving notice and sign that someone was there.

As Benny said, you had no interest in such a job no matter how high the money was.

Suddenly round the corner came an extraordinary sight. A little old man stood with prayer book in hand and started to sing. 'Onward Christian Soldiers' to the mixer-driver. Raising his feet alternately he tramped up and down in tune. Henry called out 'Here, Pop, what about singing to old Siky.' The Sikh just smiled his eternal smile and kept repeating over and over again, 'Thank you please,' thinking it was all part of the white man's mad life. Poor Siky, he was to be sacked that day. His Woolworth's trowel and level had failed to keep his corner plumb. Before the day was out his corner was kicked down and one more Bengal Lancer bit the dust. His frantic worried smile to all and sundry had only served to mark him down as a chancer.

How inoffensive the Indian is.

All round the flats new slums rose, peopled by Jews, Blacks, Indians and Arabs. For all the dirt and filth they had added something. The Jews sold Dutch herring alongside the Indian sweetmeats. Stars and crescents showed in the faces of blank windows. In the Star Café a Jamaican woman sang as she watched out for the police. A new life, a new community. Yet in all its drabness it looked in better health, as a community, than the new skyscraper flats. The new immigrants had invested the old decaying rat-trap with a feeling of strange new life. Why couldn't it be preserved. Why not rebuild and convert the old streets? Must everything become high, windy and barrack-like?

At dinner hour Henry spoke of the sea.

'Yes, I was a seaman; you know, the worst ships? The Greek boats. Do you know once I went for a job on one and the skipper says to me, "I am hand picking my crew. Let's have look at your book." Well, I thought, this is good. I had three bad discharges. Well he just looks and says, "You'll do," and he was supposed to be hand picking them.'

When the rain moved in the men just stood about idly. What did it matter? Another day gone, well, so what? Not to worry, you're a long time dead.

'Yes,' Henry says, 'I was a docker too. All my family were dockers. Do you know, during the Canadian seamen's strike we were out for fourteen weeks. Not many men would stand like that. I was with a couple of them one time during the strike. Well, we went drinking up West. That night, one of my mates says, "Let's go home to Doll, and see what she's got to eat." Well when we gets there, this geezer says to Doll, "Doll, you know that there was a meeting today of all us blokes on strike?" She says, "Yes dear, what happened?" "Well Doll, I know you can hardly believe this, but only two men out of that seven thousand voted to go back to work." His missus just looks at him. He says, "You know, Doll, who those two men were. Dick and me. But what chance did we have against that lot." Do you know, the poor old cow believed him. Dockers. I could tell you a thing or two about that lot.'

Another group chat away. Hod-carriers all. They have that lean and hardy look of men who will never be potbellied.

'You look worried, Ed.'

'So he should, dirty bastard. He has a woman up the pole.'

'Dirty, lucky bastard you mean. Going to get married, Ed?'

'Am I fuck. No. I'm too young.' He's not really. He is about twenty-four, blue-eyed, with short hair. Like all his pagan generation he wears a medal, though the God he acknowledges is not much further away than Brands Hatch.

Old Jim says, 'Well, I have been a union man all my life, though I can't say I go a lot down the branch. If you ask me all our union heads are in the pay of the master builders. Look at the general strike. I lost six weeks, and then we went back with nothing. No mate, it ain't worth studying. Married, yes. I been married. I lost my wife five years back. Miss my wife? I should say so. Thirty years of happiness. I get a little sad now and then when I pass the pub near our house. I think of the good times we had together in there. Even now of an evening I think she's there waiting for me to go home. You know when I think about her most at night, in bed, I think she's come back to me. Yes, mate, she was a good 'un. No, mate. In all those years I can truthfully say I never looked at another woman. I am getting past it now, at any rate. I'm sixty-five come October.'

Young Jim is not past it. Child of a broken marriage, he looks forward to marriage. He admits to selling purple hearts but denies he takes them. 'It's me face,' he cries, 'I know I look dopey, so I get sussed as being on drugs.' His face is a homely one; naïve, and free from any guile despite a youth spent in Borstal training. Why does he want to get married when he sees only unhappiness in his parents' efforts?

'I dunno. I just want to. She's a good girl. Can't get anything off her, though. Still, I am going to see a married bird tonight. Her old man don't want her, and yet he won't let her do what she likes, if you see what I mean.'

Next morning he looks crestfallen.

'How did you get on, Jim. Get a bit last night?'

'Did I fuck,' he shakes his head like an anxious swan. 'Her old man chased me with a chopper. He had three other blokes with him. I got out of it quick.'

Old Jim breaks in loudly with the authority of the tradesman. 'You know, it beats me. One end of the world is causing disease through these bombs, while the other is trying to cure it. It don't make sense to me.'

Our carpenter doesn't agree. A silver-haired man, handsome like an

Italian film star, he smiles. 'Don't worry about it, Jim. One good feel of woman's thigh is worth ten arguments on politics, or religion for that matter.'

'What about Ward, then. He had his share of crumpet.'

Our labourer, Dick, is a heavy, fat Jewish man.

Jim is Ward's champion. 'Well, it took a ponce to show us that a human being is stronger than them. He fucked up old Christine's plans, didn't he though? Dirty swine, they killed that man because he split on that war bloke.'

Dick laughs a heavy, fat laugh. 'You know, the history of this country is being written on the back of shit-house doors. It beats me where it's all going to end. Poor bastard, I pity him.'

A wet Friday drives us back again to the hut. Slowly the men become discontented. 'I'm jacking,' announces the Jew. 'This job is liable to give me a dose of the pox.' The others sit glumly. To leave or not to leave. All at once the whole job seems gutty. Once one man begins to go the disease spreads. By half-past eleven me and my mate decide to pull out. Maybe we will be sorry, maybe not. The general foreman, worried about head office, asks us, 'What's wrong lads? You're getting half a quid an hour and you're not pushed.' We look at him dumbly.

What's wrong? The whole thing. It's time to go. We stick our tools on our backs and pick our way gladly across the wet glistening scaffolding standing empty and dumb in the clear sun-lit rain.

CHAPTER THIRTY

Brendan

Ah Death where is thy sting a ling a ling
BRENDAN BEHAN: The Hostage

'What do I think of Brendan Behan?' The lorry driver looked worried for a minute. 'Oh I know, the big fat Irishman that was always getting drunk on tele. Well, he's a lad. Isn't he?'

Was this all there was to brother Brendan? Was he just the poor man's drunken Beatle? The crown prince of the never-ending booze-up? The press wrote big headlines that said nothing. The biggest thing about their stories was their complete lack of knowledge about Brendan. Why did he kill himself; a man who loved life? Loved to swim, play Rugby football and above all, read. Hidden behind a waterfall of beer was a man who could no longer live in a world where all the things he had fought for came to nothing. A disappointed man. Yes, disappointed in the failure of the Republican movement. Disappointed in the collapse of the left-wing world that looked upon Stalin as our father and Russia as our Mecca.

For my brother was first and foremost a rebel. He really fought for the things he believed in. And that made him different. He came out of a house that never took poverty or oppression for granted. My mother rocked him to the air of Connolly's rebel song:

> Come workers sing a rebel song,
> A song of love and hate,
> Of love unto the lowly
> And of hatred to the great.
> The great who trod our fathers down,
> Who steal our children's bread,
> Whose greedy hands are ere outstretched
> To rob the living and the dead.

My mother sang not just of hatred, but of the blessed day to come when the darkest hour would herald the brightest dawn.

Our kitchen; seven of us; my mother scrubbing and singing. Proudly she lifts her head and belts out the end of her song.

> And labour shall rise from her knees boys
> And claim the broad earth as her own.

My brother was a rebel with a thousand causes. When the Italians invaded Abyssinia, our Brendan sang, 'Will you come to Abyssinia will you come, bring your own ammunition and a gun.' When, in my ignorance, I sneered at homosexuals he turned on me like a tiger and told me to keep my dirty ignorant thoughts to myself. Although he was only fourteen when the Spanish civil war broke out he moved heaven and earth to get out there.

From the very start our Brendan was the favourite son. Good-looking with a head of dark brown curls; he easily captivated my Granny who worshipped the ground he walked on. He was to lack for nothing in a street where money was counted in halfpennies and pennies. Bengy we called him and from the start felt a little in awe of this disturbing creature who could cut you up with his tongue or his fists, as he chose. Yet running through Nature's abundant cup was a thin line of poison. For years he suffered with his nerves which caused him to stutter. He overcame this eventually but even years later when he became excited back it came. Underneath his ebullience he was a quivering mass of too much feeling. Feelings deep, raw and violent that were liable to explode at the slightest provocation. Then like a mad stallion he couldn't bear to be bridled by anyone.

He first wrote for the Republican paper *An Phoblact*. How proud I was of his work in print. Yet I remember, I fought him that night because he taunted me about my silences.

Brendan was as Dublin as the hills and loved every stone of it. On my father's side the Behans stretch back ten generations of Dublin bowsies. My granny Behan was a tenement landlady, fat, black, and powerful as any man. Thanks to the survival of the fittest the breed was short, stocky and hardy. Brendan could have lived to be ninety if he had chosen to. From my father came his love of people, from my mother his idealism. Good, uncomplicated Da, who always has a ready excuse for anyone's transgressions and in whose stubby little hands are the work of a lifetime. Fierce, wolf-like mother, who would rouse a brigade of the dead to fight for freedom. Out of these two, came Brendan. Brendan, who challenged everything to the death and then burst out laughing as he was finished doing it. Brendan, who in his youth could keep you entertained for hours acting and mimicking and making up outrageous stories about anyone he despised. One time there was a mother in the road who was driving everyone mad boasting about how she'd sent her darling boy to Lourdes to walk in the Holy procession. According to Brendan she'd sent him equipped with a pair of wooden hands, which he wore piously clasped in front, while he picked pockets with his real ones.

One of our uncles was the owner of an old Dublin music hall, The Queens. He would often send us free passes and it was great for us boys sitting in the stalls amongst all the posh customers watching plays like *The Colleen Bawn* and *Arrah na Pog*. It's small wonder that Brendan took so well to plays and playwriting.

But like everyone else he had to work for his living, and my mother's call changed from 'Brendan you'll be late for school' to 'Brendan get up for your work, your father's just going out.' He followed Da as an apprentice to the painting trade. Not just a brush hand but sign-writing and decorating. He joined the union but only attended one or two meetings. A labour republican, he saw more in direct action than long-winded resolutions. And all the while we were splitting assunder as a family. My brother Seamus was off to fight Hitler while Rory joined the free staters and supported de Valera's neutrality. I was a Marxist and looked down my nose at Republican adventurers.

One night Brendan came home to tell us that he had denounced the capitalists in his union branch for 'driving along the Stillorgan Road in their brothel wagons killing the children of the poor.' Unimpressed I poured cold water on his efforts and he went away hurt and dismayed.

Yet the family feeling has never completely dried up. It still warms my heart to remember the long letters Brendan wrote me from Borstal when I was in Malin, telling me to keep my heart up and remember it couldn't last forever.

In the intervals when we were all at home together I never saw him but he was writing. Sitting up in bed, typewriter on his knees, he never thought of food or drink till he was finished what he was doing. Then he would come down to a great bowl of soup. Worn and unshaven he looked a proper Bill Sikes.

In the main we were afraid of him. It wasn't just that he could be cruel and biting, he had an unpleasant habit of putting his finger right on the truth. So that when you had a conversation with him it was like walking in a minefield, a single lie could unleash a desperate bang.

At length he burned his paint brushes and determined to live as best he could amongst the left-bank Parisians and the arty set in Dublin. He had never had much reverence for toil. One time he was made foreman over some painters doing out a hospital. My mother sent me to pick up his money for fear it might vanish in some pub. When I got to the job I proudly asked where my brother, the foreman, might be. 'Ah,' said the painter, taking a swig at a bottle of Guinness, 'you mean Brendan man, he's one of the best. Jasus if we only had him on every job. He's out there now singing with the cleaners.' And there he was sitting on some laundry baskets between two charwomen, drunk as a monkey's uncle. He was great for organising a job of work. As the painter said, 'It's seven hours for drink and one for the work and if that interferes with the drink we'll get rid of it.'

I woke one morning to see the special police tearing our house apart. Brendan had shot a policeman and they told my father, 'Let him give himself up, Stephen, or he's a dead man.' My father, who had fought in the I.R.A. with some of the specials, pleaded with them not to plug our Brendan. Two days later Brendan was sentenced to fourteen years.

By now our house had become notorious as the local Kremlin. When Brendan came out of jail after doing about three years he found that my mother's life was being made miserable by the neighbours who were having a persecution by gossip campaign, calling her a communist cow and other such pleasantries. He soon put a stop to that by going round the streets knocking on doors and informing all and sundry that he intended having an early Guy Fawkes night and burning down the house of anyone maligning his mother. Then off we went again into the night with my mother begging him 'Brendan love, take care of yourself.' My mother was convinced by now that he was mad. Not mad in the loony sense, but mad with spirit and too much feeling that knew no bounds. Mad in the sense of too deep perceptions, of second sight almost. Mad in the sense that one minute he could be prickly and truculent and impossible to communicate with, and the next cuddly and loveable as a teddy bear.

He had a real feeling for old people. Once on a visit home I went to see my aunt Maggy Trimble. 'Ah Brian,' she said, 'your Brendan, God love him, was here yesterday in a great big car, and he nearly tore the house down knocking. "Brendan," I says, "what's wrong?" "Nothing," he shouted. "Get your coat, you and me mother are coming out for the day." "Oh Brendan," I said, "I'm too shabby, look at the cut of me, I can't ride in that big car." He only roared like the town bull. "To hell with poverty, we'll kill a chicken." And out he dragged me Brian. And away the three of us went up the mountains drinking and eating to our hearts content. Ah, God love him for thinking of an old woman.'

My mother has always had to be ready for anything. Another time he whipped her out of our kitchen, pinny and all, and the next thing she knew she was on the plane to England and a weekend at the Savoy. One night we were knocked up in the early hours to find three beautiful women bearing an unconscious Brendan into the kitchen. They laid him on the floor with all reverence while my mother ran crying round her poor cock sparrow, roundly abusing the three young women.

His friends ranged from a Dublin composer who haunted our kitchen just to hear my mother talk, to gunmen just out of jail who drank morosely and long while they talked of various nicks and mushes. When it came to ideas Brendan was always a stirring stick. He never accepted Communism, it was too cut and dried for his liking, and the idea of party discipline was anathema to him. But like many writers who came out of toil and travail he supported the Russian revolution, believing it would eventually bring world freedom. Like us all he longed for the day when we would establish a new world free from hunger and poverty. In his case it was more a longing for the big rock candy mountains, a kind of tired man's heaven. He longed to go to Russia but never made it. During the cold war the C.P. couldn't get enough tame clods to visit Russia and 'report back.' Brendan came to me and asked if I would use my influence to see that he got onto one of these cultural delegations. But the C.P. would never have risked sending him. They couldn't be sure what he would say when he came

back, and a Brendan let loose in Red Square would have hastened
Stalin's heart attack by a few years. Brendan ranted and raved about
the idiots they were sending, while real men were left behind. He was
right, all we wanted were a few castrated scribblers who would see only
what we wanted them to see. Brendan had no politics, he made them
up as he went along. He used to say the first communists were some
monks in Prague who agreed to hold everything in common long before Marx appeared on the scene.

As he became famous he was sought after by the rich and powerful,
but he was a very chancy bedfellow. Once at Dublin airport he told re-
porters that he had to go to America to earn money to support some
ignoramus in the government who couldn't tell a pig from a rabbit.

When I visited Dublin from England I never sought him out. I'd
seen him over here surrounded by what appeared to me to be syco-
phants and toadies, and I didn't want to seem to be one of them. Also I
always had a sneaking fear that he'd think I wanted to sponge on him.
Anyway it would have cost a fortune to hold your own with him when
it came to buying drinks. I wonder now if he didn't lose a lot of genuine
friends through this. Anyway he came twice to see me. Once bound-
ing up the stairs in Dublin shouting, 'Why must you live like a fucking
monk? Why can't you come out and have a drink, like anyone else?' I
started to get mad, but behind his bluster he looked so unsure and
anxious that I couldn't keep it up. Another time he descended on us
like a tornado in a Dublin street, and dragging me into the steamship
office insisted on booking first-class fares for us all back to London.

During the strike at Shell Centre, he paraded round to see all the
pickets, congratulating them on the fight and handing out money to all
and sundry. Then he marched in the gate and soundly abused the scabs
working inside. After, we went for a drink at the 'Hero of Waterloo'
and he told me, 'I'm proud of what you are doing,' and he meant it. A
blow struck, anywhere, against any oppression or injustice had his full
support. Still he felt a bit out of it with the rest of the strike committee.
Large, strong and very manly, they were completely different from
the people he had become used to drinking with. These were men you
didn't fool around with. For a while he tried pressing them to drink
with him but they politely refused. He stood silent and worried, he was
losing contact with the very people he admired. Suddenly he smiled. A

street musician came into the pub with his flute. Brendan stuffed the old man's hat with coins and notes. Then taking up the flute he dipped it in a pint of cider and slowly began playing and dancing. Out into the street he went and began begging from the passing crowds. To the old man's delight he filled the hat several times over. This was Brendan; trying to reach out through a clown's mask into the hearts of humanity.

All the while his world was crumbling. The republican movement had failed. Ten years of hunger strikes and jails and firing squads had smashed the movement that had set out to make old Ireland free. When all the world was young we thought unstinted sacrifice and fiery faith were sure to win out. But though stone walls could not a spirit break the released republican prisoners from Dartmoor and Wakefield came back to stare at empty grates or hurry to the pub to relive old battles. Time had passed them by. The clear lines of the struggle for freedom in Russia, in Spain and in Ireland were breaking up. Russian guns at Budapest were blowing the workers' paradise to hell and a grey dust was falling on all the things we had held dear.

Brendan loved humanity; he believed heart and soul in its causes. He believed in the goodness of people. But the causes crumbled and his very success drove away his true friends and left him prey to the flatterers and spongers. Fame and success became his twin headstones. The more he got the less he had. The more he drank the less he understood what had happened to his world. He became harder and harder to put up with. One night when we were celebrating the opening of *The Hostage* he suddenly turned on me and called me a traitorous bastard for leaving the Communist Party. The party he would never join himself. Even so, I know he tried hard to get a grip on things. The last time we met, that is, not surrounded by hordes of other people, he invited me out for a drink but drank nothing himself. He had a beautiful tenor voice and knew all the operas, and he just sat singing to his mother and Celia, or listening to our talk. At closing time he stood outside looking so sad and pathetic that it made me cry to look at him. He took my hand and asked me what was wrong. I couldn't speak. In any case the truth was there in his own eyes. He was done for and there was nothing he or I or anyone could do about it.

Bengy, our most favoured brother, smiled on by Nature and people, was dying. He had all the wild wilfulness of my mother, but with no

chain to bind him. Spoilt from birth by an over-abundance of talk and
flattery, he denied himself nothing. People destroy people. To make a
god of someone is to destroy them as surely as driving a knife into their
back. Our Brendan would brook no arguments as to what he did or
where and when he did it.

Self-indulgence without caring what it does to those around you can
be either selfishness or generosity, depending on where you are in the
firing line. I remember once at *The Quare Fellow* a man came up to
Brendan with his hand out saying, 'I knew you years ago.' Our Brendan loudly told him to 'fuck off out of it.' At the time I felt ill, but then
maybe he was right, at least he lived his life without compromise in
the way that he wanted to go. Perhaps the world is smaller for mingier
people like ourselves. Brendan was above all an individualist in the
extreme. A man possessed by demons that demanded absolute unques-
tioning obedience to his desires and whims. But then disillusion and
boredom set in. Struggle will never kill you, boredom will. If there's
nothing left to strive for, you collapse like a watery jelly. Standing
opposite Brendan are the thousands of lemmings who march on to their
deaths without ever doing a single thing to alter their unhappy states.
His end is preferable to their mummification. I'm damn sure a world
where the Brendans would rule would be a lot better than a crazy,
stupid, chaotic one that we live in now. In the end there was nothing
left for him to do but die, and like everything he did, he carried it to
excess.

Certainly he feared nothing, not even death whose sting he reached
out for again and again until it finished him off. He was bored: bored
with life and people. He had come to despise most of us and accused the
rest of either living in his shadow or waiting to borrow money off him.
Restlessly he went round and round and came back to nothing. Why
didn't he try writing a long novel. He was too much a person. He ex-
pressed himself in what he did and said, much more than in what he
wrote. He was too big for his own skin. A lesser man might have
peeped out at the world and made notes. Brendan jumped into it and
gave that old triangle a mighty swipe. Worse, the press began to praise
some of his stuff, even when it was rubbish. He told me 'they'd praise
my balls if I hung them high enough.' Some of his stuff he wrote now
just to pay the tax man and the bills. This seems to be the inevitable

fate of all those who write for a living. Sucked dry, they have their bones reboiled until every scrap of flesh is stripped white and clean. He wasn't writing better stuff before he died, it was getting distinctly ropey. Cut off from his main source of supply, real people, he couldn't write much about the cavorting set of false-faced bastards who praised his every belch as a sign of heavenly inspiration. But nothing or no one can take from *The Quare Fellow*, or *The Hostage*. I was very proud that my brother wrote them and that my family had added its little bit to make people laugh and cry.

Brendan was like a great storm at sea that lashes up wild waves and rocks the ships at anchor, only to spend itself in some quiet, peaceful valley. There it will drop to a quiet murmur twining its tired arms in the tall pines. Our Brendan is sleeping now, not far from the hills he loved so well. God save us from a world without room for the Brendan Behans.